DEFENSIVE FOOTBALL:
FUNDAMENTALS AND TECHNIQUES

Joe W. Gilliam, Sr.

©2002 Coaches Choice. All rights reserved. Printed in the United States.

No part of this book may be reproduced, stored in a retrieval system, or transmitted, in any form or by any means, electronic, mechanical, photocopying, recording, or otherwise, without the prior permission of Coaches Choice.

ISBN: 1-58518-596-5

Book layout: Rebecca Gold Rubin
Front cover photo: Rick Stewart/ALLSPORT
Front cover design: Rebecca Gold Rubin

Coaches Choice
P.O. Box 1828
Monterey, CA 93942
www.coacheschoice.com

DEDICATION

To the many, many defensive football players I have coached, all of whom contributed to my growth as a football coach.

ACKNOWLEDGMENTS

In my coaching career I had the good fortune, the privilege, and the opportunity to coach many magnificent defensive football players at two exceptional schools—Jackson State University in Jackson, Mississippi, and at Tennessee State University in Nashville, Tennessee. My Jackson State players included Willie Richardson, who went on to a distinguished career with the Baltimore Colts; "Speedy" Duncan of the San Diego Chargers and Washington Redskins; Ben McGee of the Super Bowl Pittsburgh Steelers; Verlon Biggs of the New York Jets and Washington Redskins; and a host of the outstanding defensive players.

Then, at Tennessee State University, I had the opportunity to work with Willie Mitchell and James Marsalis of the Super Bowl Kansas City Chiefs; Claude Humphrey and Mike Hegman of the Dallas Cowboys; Tommy Davis and King Dunlap of the Baltimore Colts; Alvin Coleman of the Minnesota Vikings and Cincinnati Bengals; Fletcher Smith of the Bengals; James "Monk" Johnson of the San Francisco 49ers; Bill Thomas, current head coach at Texas Southern University; James Greer, Don Merritt, Craig Gilliam, Waymond Bryant, and Cliff Brooks of the Cleveland Browns; Randy Fuller and Brent Alexander of the former Super Bowl champions, Pittsburgh Steelers and Atlanta Falcons.

I learned from each of these men. Willie Richardson taught me that you do not have to like tackling to become a good tackler. James Marsalis and I introduced the "bump-and-run" technique to modern-day football. Joe "Turkey" Jones, Cleveland Elam, Richard Dent and I took pass-rushing techniques to another level.

The numerous conversations I had over the years with Bill Arnsparger were most enlightening. The late Blanton Collier literally opened my eyes to the "art of tackling".

The late A.W. Mumford of Southern University in Baton Rouge, Louisiana, taught me the importance of the kicking game in football. And, there were many other players and coaches who contributed to my "education in football." To each of them, I say a sincere "thank you", for helping me to realize one of my most cherished goals, that of becoming a defensive football coach.

Chad Germany, one of my former players, has worked diligently with me in organizing and preparing this book. His associate, Anthony Dickerson is responsible for all of the computerized diagrams. To both of these men, I am eternally grateful.

Finally, I would certainly be remiss if I did not acknowledge Ms. Katisha Johns for assisting with the typing.

FOREWORD

Among the greatest "life lessons" that an individual can gain from football are those found in learning to play defense. It is on this side of the football that teamwork, team effort, single-mindedness and commitment are brought into play on every down in every game. All of these intrinsic values are absolutely necessary in order for a defensive unit to accomplish its foremost goal— "to do everything in its power to help ensure that its team wins the game."

The American way of life and the lessons learned from football are bound together. Herein lies much of the attraction that football holds for its fans, its participants, and its facilitators. The aforementioned intrinsic values must be taught by the person in charge of directing the instruction of defensive football on any and all of the different levels of play, including Pop Warner, middle school, high school, college and the professional leagues. As facilitators, coaches must "select, as to kind, and must conduct, as to outcome." In other words, coaches should expose their players to experiences in which desirable attitudes and values are developed and ingrained for life both on and off the field. All of this should be done within the context of teaching sound defensive football. As a result, the focal issue then will become a matter of what and how coaches teach. If they, as defensive facilitators, present their information, perform their on-the-field responsibilities in an appropriate manner, and exhibit a high level of integrity at all times with these values as their cornerstone, the outcomes of their coaching efforts will reflect the aforementioned values. A coach's responsibility to teach a moral and values-oriented compass in their players in an ongoing process that should be sustained on a year-round basis.

The healthy state of affairs that defensive football presently enjoys is a clear indication that many coaches are already extraordinarily good at planting the seeds of the requisite worthwhile values, and the careful nurturing of these seeds toward fruition. Throughout his career, Joe Gilliam has demonstrated values-driven leadership to both his players and those individual coaches who have had the good fortune to associate with him. His unwavering adherence to moral and ethical principles, coupled with his comprehensive knowledge of the game, has enabled him to be a role model for all of us.

Bill Arnsparger

CONTENTS

Dedication   3
Acknowledgements   4
Foreword   11
Preface   13
Diagram Key   14

Chapter 1 – DEFENSIVE PHILOSOPHY   15

- The origin of a defense philosophy
- A winning defensive philosophy
- Down linemen
- Inside linebackers
- Defensive backs
- The entire defense

Chapter 2 – TACKLING   19

- Fear control
- Fundamentals of tackling
- Tackling evaluation
- Passive tackling
- Tackling drills

Chapter 3 – DOWN LINEMEN   28

- Blocker control
- Eight basic techniques to control blockers:

    | ✓ Technique I | ✓ Technique V |
    | ✓ Technique II | ✓ Technique VI |
    | ✓ Technique III | ✓ Technique VII |
    | ✓ Technique IV | ✓ Technique VIII |

- Essentials for a good pass rusher

Chapter 4 – LINEBACKERS 35
- Blitzing linebackers
- Defending the run:
    - ✓ Blocker control
    - ✓ Keying
    - ✓ Defensive team – option/outside run responsibilities
- Defending the pass:
    - ✓ Sprint-out coverage for linebackers
    - ✓ Man coverage for linebackers

Chapter 5 – DEFENSIVE BACKS 43
- Defending against the run:
    - ✓ Blocker control
    - ✓ Tackling
    - ✓ Option support
    - ✓ Playing down and distance
    - ✓ Regular keys
- Defending against the pass:
    - ✓ Back peddling
    - ✓ Cushioning
    - ✓ Masking coverages
    - ✓ Pass defense zones
    - ✓ Zone coverages on dropback passes
    - ✓ Covers and assignments vs. QB roll-out
    - ✓ Man coverage
    - ✓ Defensive back drills

Chapter 6 – TAKE AWAY THE RUN FIRST ... 70
- Make the offense one-dimensional
- Defending reverses and misdirection
- The box
- Down linemen and linebackers vs. blocking schemes
- Defending option teams
- Combining odd and even fronts
- Secondary adjustments to motion and spread alignments
- Entire defenses
- Defensive team practice
- Demonstration (scout) team

Chapter 7 – RED ZONE DEFENSE ... 86
- Red zone attitude
- Tighten-up, load-up, and blitz
- Suggested defenses from the 22-yard line to the 10-yard line
- Suggested defenses from the 10-yard line to the 4-yard Line
- Suggested defenses from the 4-yard line to the goal line

Chapter 8 – DESIGNING AN EFFECTIVE RUNNING PROGRAM ... 91
- Making the defenders faster:
    - ✓ General ways to improve speed
    - ✓ A resistance program for developing speed
    - ✓ Speed training
- A recommended running program for defensive players
- Preparing to run for time
- Suggested preparation routine
- Guidelines for conducting time trials

Chapter 9 – WEIGHT TRAINING PROGRAM 99
- Discoveries
- The recommended program
- Locating the "proper starting point"
- Increasing the amount of weight lifted
- Proper lifting techniques
- Lifting sessions
- The lifting sequence

Chapter 10 – THE WINNING EDGE 107
- An awesome responsibility
- Great work ethic plus great focus plus highly drilled players equals the winning edge

Appendix 109
About the Author 110

PREFACE

This book begins with a discussion of defensive philosophy, emphasizing that this philosophy should be "tentative" because it will undergo changes before an approach is decided upon. Constant change is probably a good sign of philosophic improvement. Realizing that there is no perfect approach to defensive play, and that offensive innovations force the defense to face the old adage, "either change with the times or stand to be consumed by the times."

There is a special emphasis on the need and value of, "drilling the skills," because it is through repetition that potential becomes a realization. There is also the basic approach that the parts and assignments in your defensive scheme should be broken down into drills so that almost all of your drills are "mini-parts" of your defensive scheme.

A portion of this work is devoted to tackling—the "cornerstone" of effective defensive play. Overcoming the pain/injury factor in tackling is the first step in becoming an outstanding tackler. The basic approach is to start with "passive" tackling drills and then move to "live" tackling drills with the premise that it is more effective to teach in a "passive" setting. Then, use "live" tackling drills, at times, as an "exam" in tackling.

The chapter involving basic secondary play and Cover 3 contains several innovative ideas and skills. We have found Cover 3 to be an excellent coverage that is extremely difficult to scout and to devise an attack-scheme against.

A unique feature of the alignment-change from an, "odd-front to an even-front," is the use of the "big end", often referred to as an elephant linebacker. It is important to note that the change can be accomplished with little change in assignments. The "big end" forced the blocking innovation of "big-on-big", (a lineman, not a back, blocking on the "big end"). The college careers of Joe "Turkey" Jones, Cleveland Elam, and Richard Dent helped to force the blocking innovation of "big-on-big" that is still used to a great extent in pass protection.

Generally, defensive materials do not include a complete running program. The originality of this concept of cardio-vascular conditioning and other intrinsic benefits makes this book an important tool for defensive coaches.

I have never seen a defensive football book that included a complete suggested weight program. The weight program information included in this book provides an additional source of valuable coaching information.

DIAGRAM KEY

Symbols

○ — Offensive player
□ — Offensive center
◐ — Offensive player's shade
--▶ — Direction or pathway of a player

Abbreviations

BC — Ballcarrier
DB — Defensive back
DE — Defensive end
DT — Defensive tackle
FL — Flanker
FS — Free safety
ILB — Inside linebacker
LB — Linebacker
LDB — Left defensive back
LOS — Line of scrimmage
LSS — Left strong safety
MDB — Middle defensive back
MLB — Middle linebacker
NB — Near back

NG — Nose guard
OLB — Outside linebacker
POA — Point of attack
QB — Quarterback
RDB — Right defensive back
RSS — Right strong safety
S — Safety
SE — Split end
SILB — Strong inside linebacker
SS — Strong safety
ST — Strong tackle
T — Tackle
TE — Tight end
WILB — Weak inside linebacker

CHAPTER 1

DEFENSIVE PHILOSOPHY

THE ORIGIN OF A DEFENSIVE PHILOSOPHY

The first ingredient in the recipe of developing a powerful defense is to establish a tentative philosophy. The emphasis is on "tentative" because a coach's defensive philosophy will typically undergo quite a few changes and alterations while becoming one that really works for that individual.

A person's philosophy provides that individual with a tenet-based guideline, a source of direction, if you will, a reservoir of premises, principles, ideas and temporary beliefs that help an individual decide what to so in a particular situation. Webster's Dictionary defines a philosophy as "a discipline with logic and ethics as its core; it also includes general beliefs, attitudes and concepts of an individual or group." The encyclopedia further states that "the purpose of a philosophy is two-fold:"

- It tries to give a person a unified view of something.
- It seeks to make a person a more "critical thinker".

The great American philosopher, John Dewey, once stated that learning is a result of a person's experiences (pragmatic) and, as a consequence, an individual's philosophy should be and probably is dynamic. In that regard, a coach's philosophy provides him with a conceptual blueprint for action. In other words, a coach's philosophy is often the single most important influence on how he coaches.

A WINNING DEFENSIVE PHILOSOPHY

Developing a "philosophy" is important because an individual's thoughts, beliefs, actions and approaches to football are guided by his philosophy. If coaches, in fact, learn from their experiences, it then stands to reason that good football experiences breed good football players. And conversely, poor football experiences breed poor football players, not withstanding the inclusion of talent. The coach is the "director" of all of this, and as such, has the unique opportunity to present situations from which good football experiences can emanate.

Furthermore, a defensive player's attitude and thinking must be one of seriousness and resolute commitment to team goals because one of the primary purposes of defense is immense—to see to it that their team does not lose the game. Regardless of how many points that an opponent may score, the defense has accomplished the team's primary goal if their team simply does not lose the game. Coaches should always keep in mind because the primary goal of an offensive team is to score points, to a great degree, the defense carries the brunt of the responsibility in determining whether its team loses or wins.

One critical aspect of a defensive coach's philosophy concerns the use of drills. It is virtually impossible for the defense to achieve their intended objectives unless they drill on a regular basis. Considerable evidence supports the fact that the buildup of good execution enhances the development of essential skills. In that regard, it is important to remember that. To drill ten minutes of drill for five days is more beneficial, in the learning process, than to drill one day for fifty minutes. Practice continuity is another factor that needs to be considered.

Perhaps the most meaningful and productive drills are actual parts of a team's defensive system, broken down into individual or unit techniques and assignments, and performed repeatedly. As a result, a defensive player's skills, techniques, and assignments become almost "second nature." Through proper drilling, the beginning player, whether on the high school or college level, can become a more skilled player. Furthermore, the upperclassman can become a more seasoned and accomplished player. In fact, even professional players could also improve their performance by engaging in drills more often.

In reality, a coach is missing the "big picture" if he believes that just being on the team, scrimmaging, reviewing assignments, and playing the games is the most efficient way to develop or improve a player's technique and skills. Repetition (drilling) of skills, techniques and assignments has long been known to drastically reduce mistakes. The renowned John Wooden, believed strongly in muscle repetition, (i.e., drilling as a wonderful way of developing and/or improving skills).

Another essential area of a defensive coach's philosophy involves the use of defensive fronts. When a defense presents both odd fronts (three-man, five-man, seven-man fronts) and even fronts (four-man, six-man, eight-man fronts), an opponent's preparation for these schemes increases immeasurably. The "trick" is to develop a defensive system that employs both odd and even fronts, but does not overload the assignments for defensive players unlike the situation that offensive players often face. If a defensive coach has ever been an offensive player or coach, he can clearly see the monumental task that an offensive line coach has in preparing to meet a team that utilizes odd and even fronts. Similarly, that same defensive coach generally has insight into how offensive coaches and quarterbacks can best attack his defenses.

Yet another important factor in a defensive coach's philosophy involves having and exhibiting a steadfast sense of self-assurance. They should like what they do, and be good at it. Furthermore, they should have high expectations of themselves and their players. They should be able to instill a belief within their players, that the approach they are using will produce well-trained players who collectively will combine to become a powerful defense. This "approach," advocated by each individual coach, has its basis in the following principles:

DOWN LINEMEN MUST:

- Develop an exceptional level of physical strength.
- Be quick and agile.
- Assume a stance that will facilitate the movements they must make.
- Watch the weight on the offensive man's down-hand. If his weight is heavy and his heels are off the ground, he is coming forward. If the blocker's weight is light on his down hand and his heels are near the turf, he plans to move laterally or pass block.
- Always put their pads and hands under the blocker's pads and roll their hips forward when making contact with their blockers.
- Always work to "slide the front of the blocker" rather than go around the "back door" when making contact.
- Never allow the blocker to "ride" them beyond the passer when they're rushing the passer. When the blocker is the same depth as the passer, they roll to the inside toward the quarterback.
- Straight-arm shiver in a downward fashion, while simultaneously chopping their feet to keep the blocker away from their feet if a blocker is below their knees.
- Step into a post-blocker with their inside foot and "feel" his block when fighting the double-team block. If the block is a double-team, they should duck their head low into the lead blocker to prevent movement, or get into the seam between the blockers and fight the pressure of lead blocker to prevent movement.
- Never allow the blocker to get into their chest when rushing the passer.

- Always attack one-half of the blocker if they are not using a bull-rush technique while rushing the passer. They can attack either the outside half or the inside half, but cannot allow blocker to "center-up" on you.
- Never back away from contact and, in general, seek to intimidate their opponents through rough, aggressive contact at every opportunity.
- Tighten-down off a blocker's butt and look for a block inside-out if he crosses their face.
- Flex (i.e., back off the line-of-scrimmage about three feet), if they are being successfully double-teamed, in order to give themselves more time to see the double-team block and properly react to it.

INSIDE LINEBACKERS MUST:

- Keep outside leverage on the ballcarrier (frontside linebacker) in a two-way linebacker alignment, while keeping "cut-back" leverage on the ballcarrier (the backside linebacker).
- Shuffle until they reach the tackle hole in order to be on balance when taking on blockers or defending the cut-back of the ballcarrier.
- Shuffle until they reach the tackle hole so as to be on balance when taking on blockers / the cut-back of the ballcarrier.
- Watch for "trash" and slip blocks when shuffling across double-team blocks. They should not press into the line-of-scrimmage.
- Move up into the offensive hole and put their pads under lead blocker's pads, stand him up, shed him and either make the tackle or drive the lead blocker into the ballcarrier.
- Run sideways on pass drop, getting at least eight yards wide and eight yards deep and count; on the formation side, look tight end, flanker, or near back; on the split-end side, look for the split end, near back, or across (the crossing receiver).

DEFENSIVE BACKS MUST:

- Focus on their key to quickly determine whether the play is a run or a pass and if they are the "force man" on wide runs.
- Get across the line of scrimmage into offensive backfield at an outside-in angle if they are focusing a wide run. If the ballcarrier is close to his blocker, they should go into the blocker low and hard in an

attempt to take both of them down. If there is space between the two, they should take on the blocker with their hands or shoulder, and keep their feet in order to "shed" the blocker and make the tackle.

- Attack the ballcarrier as soon as their key indicates run if they are a safety.

- Watch the receiver closely; dog him, bump him, and generally harass him, if he runs a good pattern and gives them trouble.

- Assume an inside "hip-pocket" technique and run with the receiver if he "breaks the defensive back's cushion."

- Watch the lace of his pants when covering a receiver. When the lace drops, prepare for the receiver to fake or make a cut.

- Always take away the receiver's inside pass-cuts first, thereby forcing longer passes and thus reducing completion percentages.

- Stay on balance and run under control as long as the receiver is in front of them.

- Quickly get a position directly behind the receiver after he makes his cut and keep this position until the ball arrives.

- Watch both the receiver and the passer until the ball is thrown, after the receiver makes his cut.

- Go to the ball once it is thrown (all defenders).

- Play pass first and run second on all downs.

- Always "take-away two". Whether the defender is in zone or man coverage, the receiver has three basic directions he can go: straight up (fly), out, or in. By his very position on the receiver, the defender should always take-away the fly first and then the in or out pattern. Since the defender knows where he is most vulnerable, he can anticipate a cut in that direction and more quickly defend his weakness.

- Always know from which direction they can expect "help" in their coverage.

- Possess a high level of cardiovascular conditioning because of the tremendous amount of running and movement required of a defensive back.

THE ENTIRE DEFENSIVE UNIT MUST:

- Be the aggressor.
- Be an offensive-oriented defense.
- Be relentless in pursuing the ballcarrier until the whistle blows.
- Always give a "maximum effort".
- Play fearlessly; look for and welcome contact.
- Lead, do not counter unless necessary.
- Always play "down-and-distance".
- Feel the responsibility of the "defense" to make sure the team does not lose the game.
- Be aware of the fact that if the opponent moves the ball on the ground against them they are getting "out hit".
- Take away the opponent's ability to run the football first; then; the game becomes "one dimensional" and easier for the defense to play.
- Set a pace-of-play that tends to tire-out the offense by the fourth quarter.
- Work hard and be serious in the weight room, because this effort will enable them to be better able to withstand the intense contact a defensive player generally encounters without sustaining serious injury.
- Be ready to handle pass, screen, and draw on all passing situations.
- Remember that a defensive team will play better or worse each performance, depending upon their preparation, motivation, and their inward desire to excel. But they will never play the "same" as in their last performance, because "nothing that is dynamic stays the same."
- Understand that repetition (drilling) assures player growth and greater success. It is in this context that confidence and poise are enhanced in well-drilled players.

CHAPTER 2

TACKLING

The rule-makers of football have never legislated against how hard a player can hit, but rather where a player can hit the ballcarrier. Apparently the rule-makers intended to allow hard hitting (i.e., hard tackling).

FEAR CONTROL

It is erroneous to think that an appreciable number of defensive players do not, at one time or another, harbor a fear of pain/injury during the execution of a tackle. On the contrary, when focusing on tackling during a game or during the viewing of tackling on videos, the fear of injury clearly, "comes and goes" throughout games and scrimmages. In fact, it appears that many missed tackles and poor tackles can legitimately be attributed to the inability of players to properly control their fear of being injured while making a tackle. Intuitively, almost every player realizes that his fear of pain/injury is not an acceptable reason for tackling poorly or missing tackles.

A defensive coach can play an enormous role in teaching players to properly control their fear of being injured while tackling, or remove such a fear entirely. In this regard, every player must be taught that his fear of being injured is a totally unacceptable reason for missing a tackle or making a poor tackle, and, such reasoning will never, ever be acceptable. This premise must be emphasized over and over again in all tackling situations. A coach must teach a tackling technique that will minimize the chances of a defender being injured. And maximize accuracy. Additionally, the defensive coach should drill his players by initially tackling passively, and then by tackling live on a regular basis in order to develop good tackling technique. Furthermore, the coach should evaluate all tackling in both practice and games. It should be strongly emphasized to the players that the fear of injury is understandable but it must be either controlled properly or eliminated altogether if they ever envision being good defensive football players on a sound defensive team.

FUNDAMENTALS OF TACKLING

The "fundamental football position" is the starting point for successful tackling. This position involves adherence to the following factors:

- Feet:
    - ❑ Spread feet to slightly less then shoulder-width apart.
    - ❑ Position the feet parallel to each other, pointing straight upfield.
    - ❑ Keep the weight forward on the balls of the feet.
- Body (the "body angles" should be as near to 45 degrees as possible):
    - ❑ Bend at the knees.
    - ❑ Close the waist angle.
    - ❑ Close the angle between the top of the feet and front of the lower shins.
    - ❑ Arch the back in order to tense all muscles for hitting.
    - ❑ Raise the head to see the arms and hands of the opponent.
    - ❑ Let the arms dangle loosely between the legs or in the knee area.
    - ❑ Ball the fist and turn the knuckles so that the back of the hand faces the line-of-scrimmage.
- Eyes-on-numbers (note: because the jersey numbers are the slowest moving and the softest part of the ballcarrier, keeping the eyes on the ballcarrier's numbers enhances tackling accuracy and encourages hard tackling):
    - ❑ Assume the "fundamental football position."
    - ❑ Take a short jab-step with arms in a "shoot" position to explode into the ball-carrier (keeping the eyes open throughout contact).
    - ❑ Grab the back of the ballcarrier's thigh, while simultaneously pulling him up and into your body.
    - ❑ Drive the ballcarrier backward into the ground, landing on top of him with your head and face digging deep into his chest area.
    - ❑ Do not turn the ballcarrier loose until after landing on the turf.
    - ❑ Always execute the "eyes-on-numbers" technique the same way, regardless of where you are on the field and the angle in which you approach the ballcarrier.

TACKLING EVALUATION

Evaluating a skill, such as tackling, can take a positive direction as well as a negative direction. It is a plus when a coach can motivate a player to great effort and achievement by showing a player how he is progressing. Conversely, the same can be said when the player is retrogressing. Keep in mind that as a rule, most players generally respond better to praise than to criticism. In developing tackling skills, a player must buy into the concept "practice makes perfect". It is unrealistic to expect players to maintain or improve their tackling skill if their only tackling opportunities occur during the game. On the contrary, a player should perform passive tackling drills daily, and live tackling drills several times a week. If preventing injuries becomes a factor, it is advisable to close the distance between the tackler and the ballcarrier to two or three yards, thereby reducing velocity of the collision between the "ballcarrier" and the tackler, and lessening the potential for injuries to occur.

A passive tackling evaluation should include the following factors:

- The eyes are open at the moment of contact.
- The tackler utilizes proper hand placement and body positioning.
- The "snatch" movement is prevalent. (A perfect score would be a three; average = two; poor = one).

A live tackling evaluation should include the following factors:

- The eyes are open at the moment of contact.
- The tackler utilizes proper hand placement and body positioning.
- The tackler "unloads" into the ball carrier.
- The "snatch" movement is prevalent.
- The tackler still has the ballcarrier in his grasp when they land on the ground. (A perfect score would be four; good = three; average = two; poor = one or none).

At the end of a practice-week, the daily evaluations should be totaled and presented to the defensive squad. A running record of the defenders' tackling efforts on a game-by-game, as well as a seasonal basis should also be kept.

PASSIVE TACKLING

When teaching any contact skill, it is advisable to introduce the players to the skill in a non-contact setting (passive). As a result, the techniques can be taught and learned without the potential distraction of pain and/or injury to the learning process. During a passive tackling session, the coach should focus on the tackler's body position, hand position, and head position with the eyes open at contact "If you want to miss, close your eyes." Diagrams 2.1 and 2.2 illustrate two passive tackling drills that cover almost any situation a defensive player might encounter. Passive tackling should be drilled every day by all defensive players.

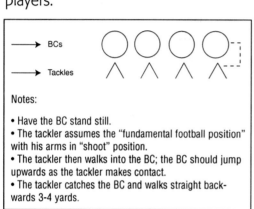

Diagram 2.1. Head-on tackling. **Diagram 2.2. Angle right and left tackling.**

TACKLING DRILLS

A tackling drill, conducted in either a passive or live fashion, can be attached to the end of any instructional or development drill whether that drill is an agility and quickness drill, a skill drill, or a technique drill. All factors considered, it is more appropriate to attach passive tackling drills to the end of agility and quickness drills, and live tackling drills to the end of skill drills and technique drill. Diagram 2.3 through 2.18 illustrate examples of tackling drills that can be utilized with down linemen, linebackers, and defensive backs.

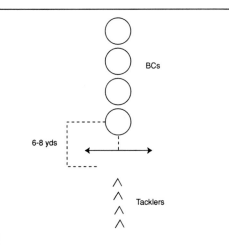

Notes:
• The BC starts straight at the tackler and cuts at a 90° degree angle either right or left.
• The tackler moves straight at the BC and comes under control, he then moves toward the BC with his arms in a chute position and shadows the BC for several steps, but doesn't not make contact with him.
• The BC jumps upward as the tackler moves to make contact.

Points of emphasis:
• Keep eyes focused on the BCs jersey number.
• Maintain proper body position and hands placement.
• Put nose-on-chest; lift and pull the BC into your body.

Diagram 2.3. Shadow drill.

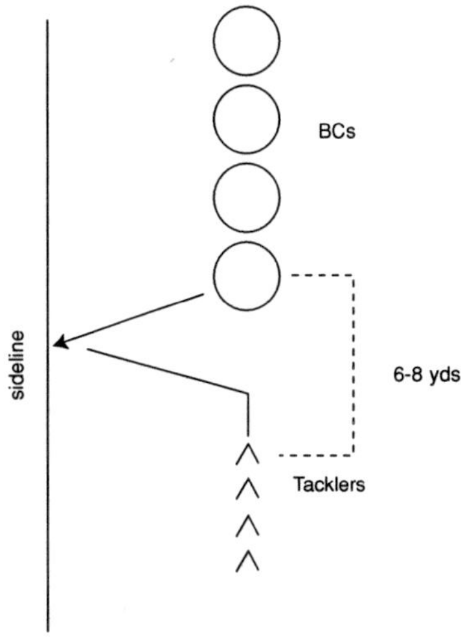

Notes:
• The BC starts running into the sideline; the BC has the option of continuing down the sideline or cutting back toward the middle of the field.
• The tackler runs straight ahead for a few yards (this "up" movement should take away the BCs cutback); the tackler then angles into the sideline to trap the BC against the sideline — aiming slightly to the middle of BC
• The BC jumps as the tackler makes contact.

Points of emphasis:
• Keep eyes open and focused on the target (the BC's jersey number).
• Maintain proper body position.
• Put nose-on-chest; lift and pull the BC into your body.

Diagram 2.4. Sideline drill.

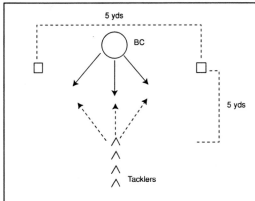

Notes:
• The BC can take any one of these directions (as shown in diagram).
• The tackler moves forward, comes under control, and makes a chute, while keeping his head up and eyes open.
• The tackler shadows the BC but does not make contact.

Points of emphasis:
• Keep the body under control while executing an open-field tackle.
• Using proper movement mechanics, perform an "up" angle.
• Maintain proper head and hand placement.
• Keep eyes open.

Diagram 2.5. Breakout drill.

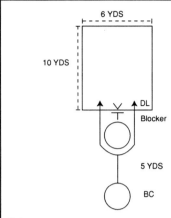

Notes:
• The blocker starts at his discretion (no starting count is used).
• The drill starts again at the point the DL made the tackle.
• The procedure is repeated for three downs or 10 yds. whichever comes first (this method will stimulate competitiveness).

Diagram 2.6. "Bloody alley" linemen's drill.

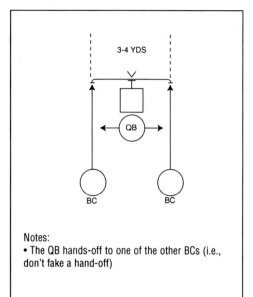

Notes:
• The QB hands-off to one of the other BCs (i.e., don't fake a hand-off)

Diagram 2.7. "Control and tackle" drill.

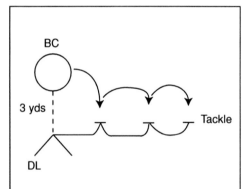

Notes:
• The BC and DL butt each other two times; and on the third time the DL tackles the BC

Points of emphasis:
• The DL focuses on maintaining outside leverage on the BC
• The DL executes a "nose-on-numbers" tackle.

Diagram 2.8. "Butt and tackle" drill.

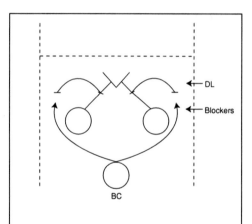

Notes:
• The blockers fire-out on the DL, one-at-a-time, not following-through.
• The DL steps into the blockers.
• The ricochet is used more on "gap defenses".

Points of emphasis:
• The DL steps outside each blocker, sticking his face mask and hands under the blocker's pads.
• The DL sheds the blocker and slides the face of blocker, squares-up and executes a "nose-on-numbers" tackle.

Diagram 2.9. "Ricochet" drill.

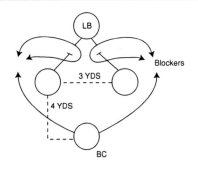

Notes: The LB assumes the fundamental football position.
• The purpose of the drill is to teach the LB to beat the block-down of OL or TE.
• The coach should signal whom he wants to block the LB.

Points of emphasis:
• The LB shuffles, keeping shoulders square to the LOS.
• The BC fakes toward the LOS or toward his own backfield; he then attacks either the outside shoulders or the inside shoulder of the blocker with his inside or outside shoulder.
• The LB sheds to blocker, slides, squares-up and executes a "nose-on-numbers" tackle.

Diagram 2.10. "Lone ranger" drill.

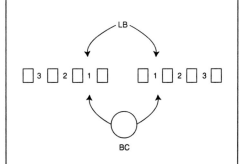

Notes:
• The purpose of the drill is for the LB to work on his shuffling technique, squaring up in the holes and executing a "nose-on-numbers" tackle.

Diagram 2.11. "The eye opener" drill.

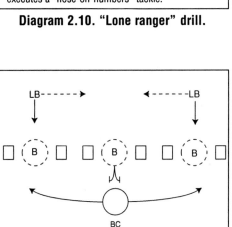

Notes:
• The purpose of the drill is to teach shuffling and taking-on-blockers in or near the offensive hole, shedding, "stuffing" the blocker and making the tackle or clogging-up the hole.

Points of emphasis:
• The LB must move up into the hole, shed or "stuff" the blocker, and execute a "nose-on-numbers" tackle.
• If the ball is "away," The LB must shuffle, take on the blocker, shed the blocker, and aid in the tackle.

Diagram 2.12. "Back the line" drill.

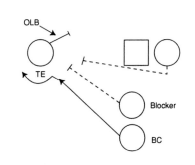

Notes:
• The purpose of the drill is to teach the OLB to close-off the tackle hole and make the tackle if possible.

Points of emphasis:
• On the snap, the OLB steps into the TE.
• If the TE goes down inside, the OLB will close off the TE, but keep his shoulders parallel to LOS and meet the blocker (TE or OG) low with the side of his shoulder pads, elbows and knees.

Diagram 2.13. "Road block" drill.

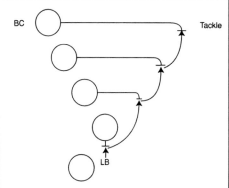

Notes:
- The blockers each throw one scramble block at the legs of the OLB in succession.

Points of emphasis:
- The OLB stands-up the first blocker, sheds him, and moves out and up to next blocker, while keeping their feet moving.
- The OLB repeats same blocker-control, only focus on their hand placement on the next blocker.
- The OLB squares-up and executes a "nose-on-numbers" tackle.

Diagram 2.14. "Ward off" drill.

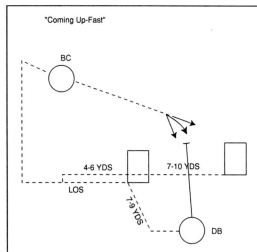

Notes:
- The drill starts on the movements of the BC
- The BC runs anywhere between the two dummies.

Points of emphasis:
- The DB forces from an outside-in angle across the LOS into the offensive backfield.
- The DB comes under control (break down while staying-in-motion).
- The DB focuses on the BC's belt buckle and executes a "nose-on-numbers" tackle.

Diagram 2.16. Control and tackle drill.

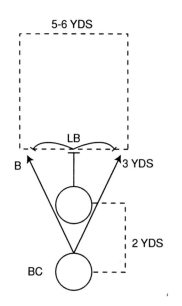

Notes:
- The purpose of this drill is to teach LBs to "take-on" blockers and make the tackle.

Points of emphasis:
- The LB "takes-on" the blocker by sticking his face mask and both hands under the blocker's pads.
- The LB sheds or "stuffs" the blocker into the BC, and executes a "nose-on-numbers" tackle.

Diagram 2.15. "Bloody alley for Linebackers" drill.

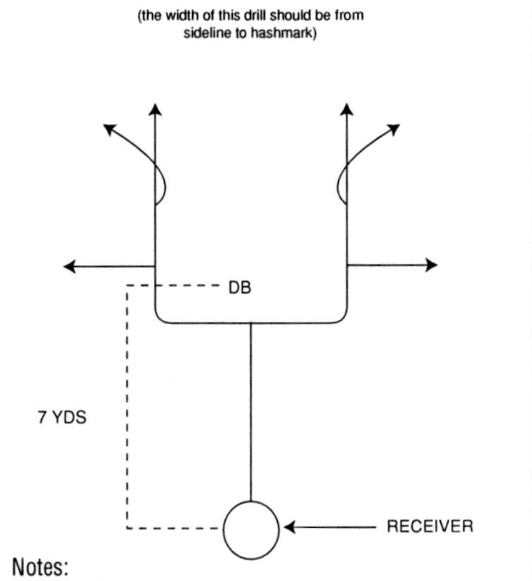

(the width of this drill should be from sideline to hashmark)

7 YDS

RECEIVER

Notes:
• The DB begins on his stomach.
• The receiver runs any pattern he desires over 7 yds.
• The DB defends the pass-line.

Points of emphasis:
• The DB quickly jumps to his feet and "breaks down" under control.
• The focus of the DB is on the belt buckle of the receiver; when the buckle drops, the DB prepares for a cut or fake.
• The DB should play to intercept, knock the pass down, or make the tackle.

Diagram 2.17. "Twilight zone" drill.

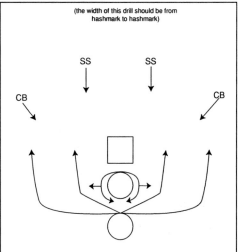

Notes:
• The QB and BC can make any movement or go any direction they desire.
• On the snap, the secondary take their usual step-or-two backward to the ball.

Points of emphasis:
• The DBs locate the direction of the BC and pursue in a "trapping" fashion with an awareness of the BC and their secondary teammates.
• The DBs gang tackle the BC

Diagram 2.18. "Gang up" drill.

CHAPTER 3

DOWN LINEMEN

BLOCKER CONTROL

Blocker control is as vital to defensive football as tackling, running, and general aggressiveness. Defensive coaches often emphasize, "not staying blocked" to their players, because defeating the block has to be the primary priority in teaching defensive play. This skill should be taught to all defensive positions. If offensive players can block the defenders, their plays will likely be successful; and if their plays are successful, they will usually win. Therefore, one of the skills taught to down linemen and linebackers should involve techniques to prevent offensive players from blocking them, (i.e., "blocker control").

EIGHT BASIC TECHNIQUES TO CONTROL BLOCKERS

Defensive linemen must be taught methods to control the blocker, or ways to keep blockers away from their bodies so that they can quickly get to the point-of-attack. However, when a blocker does get into the defender's body, the defender must know how to get extension on the blocker, shed him (throw the blocker off his body), and pursue the tackle the ballcarrier.

In defensive jargon, the word "technique" often means "alignment position". For example, a 6 technique is generally thought to be a point somewhere between the offensive tackle and the offensive end. In this book, however, the definition of "technique" means "a specific maneuver". It is in this context that the "eight basic techniques" emerge. The recommended procedure is to teach the eight techniques to down linemen, and then assign each lineman a "technique" when he's placed in a defensive scheme. This way, a coach can then use multiple fronts with a minimum number of assignments.

In this regards, a lot of practice time involves a constant repetition of the same eight basic skills. Since the linemen have fewer assignments to master, they should quickly become more proficient and quicker in their ability to effectively perform these techniques. Fortunately, repetitions accumulate at a tremendous rate.

Technique I: (Used when a defender covers any portion of an offensive lineman.)

In this technique, on the first offensive blocker movement, the defender charges into the blocker (i.e., hit first, don't "be hit") by using a two-hand, straight-arm upward shiver into the chest of the blocker, while simultaneously sticking his face mask into his chin. Then, the defender rolls his hips forward and rolls his elbows inward in order to lock his elbows (i.e., get separation from the blocker). These two movements should propel the blocker upward and away, thereby reducing his power as a blocker. The defensive player should keep his feet moving quickly throughout this maneuver, while locating the direction of either the ball carrier or the blocker who wants to take him. He then sheds the blocker and pursues to tackle the ballcarrier. If the blocker goes down across defender's face, he tightens off his butt and looks for a trap. If the blocker pulls, the defender goes with him, looking for a block from that direction. He then either slides across-the-face of the blocker or back/door the block. (Refer to Diagram 3.1)

Technique II: (Used when the blocker attacks at knees or below. Also, this technique "overrides" the originally assigned technique.)

In this technique, the defensive player straight-arm-shivers the blocker in a downward direction, locking his hands into the blocker, rotate his elbows inward, and lifting his feet in a rapid, chopping fashion, while keeping the blocker away from his legs and reading the direction of the blocker's head. He then sheds him and pursues to the point-of-attack. If the blocker goes down across the defender's face, he tightens off his butt and looks for a trap. If the blocker pulls, the defender trails him, looking for a block from a player in the direction of puller. The defender then "slides" that block or "back doors" that block. (Refer to Diagram 3.2)

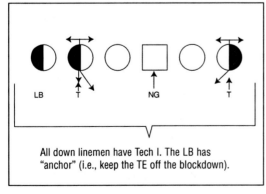

All down linemen have Tech I. The LB has "anchor" (i.e., keep the TE off the blockdown).

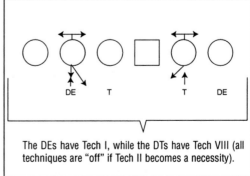

The DEs have Tech I, while the DTs have Tech VIII (all techniques are "off" if Tech II becomes a necessity).

Diagram 3.1. Tech I (basic odd front).   **Diagram 3.2. Tech II.**

Technique III: (Used when playing gap-control defense.)

In this technique, the defensive player backs off the line-of-scrimmage a foot or two in order to reduce the acuteness of the blocker's angle. He steps down the middle of the stance of the blocker to his immediate outside, delivering hid near shoulder and both hands into the blocker, his pads under the blocker's pads. If the defender gets blocked, he must do one of three things: attempt to "slide" the face of the blocker if blocker has out-positioned him, by flattening out and driving him in that direction; spin out and pursue; or drop the shoulder closest to the blocker and "back door" him (i.e., go around the blocker and pursue the ballcarrier in a trailing mode). (Refer to Diagram 3.3)

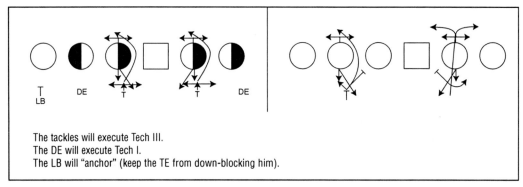

The tackles will execute Tech III.
The DE will execute Tech I.
The LB will "anchor" (keep the TE from down-blocking him).

Diagram 3.3. Tech III.

Technique IV: (Used when gaps widen or on short yardage/passing situations.)

In this technique, the defender tightens to inside-most spot of the gap. The greatest immediate danger to him comes from the "block down" (outside). He aligns as close to the line-of-scrimmage as possible without being offside. He then works to "fly" through the gap for penetration by either dropping the shoulder closest to outside blocker (as he flies through the gap) or thrust both of his arms vigorously forward in a swinging upward fashion with both fists clenched tightly as he works to burst the gap (the arm thrusting helps to remove blocking surface.) Once the line-of-scrimmage has been penetrated, he sharply "breaks-it-off" and pursues the ballcarrier from behind to make the tackle. If the outside blocker does not block on him, he tightens to the inside and looks immediately for an impending inside-out block. If one comes, he drops low, braces and fights pressure. If no block from outside or inside occurs, he closes inside fast and sets for a trap block. (Refer to diagram 3.4)

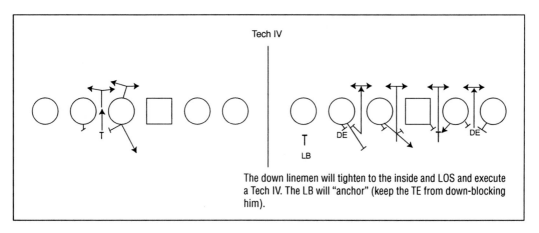

Diagram 3.4. Tech IV.

Technique V: (A stunt used to nullify the opponent as a blocker and on short-yardage situations.)

In this technique, the defensive player fires through the blocker to his immediate inside or outside (depending upon the assignment) with great velocity and power in order to cave the blocker in, thereby rendering him ineffective as a blocker. If the blocker to the outside blocks down on him, he dips the shoulder nearest that blocker and proceeds in the back door. If no one blocks on him, he sets for a trap or ballcarrier. (Refer to Diagram 3.5)

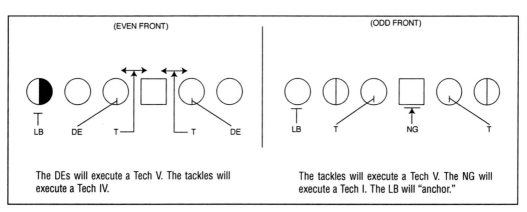

Diagram 3.5. Tech V.

Technique VI: (Used in definite passing situations.)

In this technique, the lineman squeezes the LOS, assumes a sprinter's stance, and executes his best pass-rush technique. Note: unless he is using a "bull-rush" technique, he should work only one-half of a blocker. If there is no block on him or a very poor block, he should "smell a rat" (i.e., screen or draw).

Technique VII: (Used to break down blocking schemes.)

This technique involves a looping maneuver that is executed with a quick, lateral step; immediately followed by a forward movement. The defenders' shoulders should be parallel to the line-of-scrimmage throughout the maneuver. If the loop is directed toward the left, the defensive players to the left of the offensive center should make their lateral (lead) step with their left foot in order to be able to instantly pursue if the point-of-attack is to their side.

The defensive players to the right of the center should make their first step with their right foot (crossover), while thrusting their right arm in the same direction to take away the blocking surface. The crossover step assures a better base on the second step if the blocker makes contact as the defender crosses. It also affords better footwork if the play is going in the opposite direction of the "loop". When the loop is directed toward the right, these movements are simply reversed. After executing a loop, either to the left or to the right, the defender closes to the inside for the trap if he doesn't feel any pressure. (Refer to Diagram 3.6)

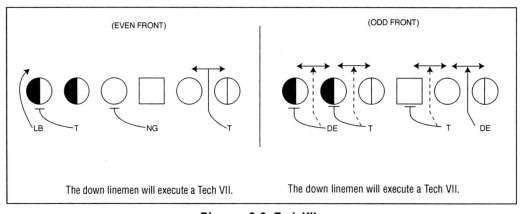

Diagram 3.6. Tech VII.

Technique VIII: (Used from an "over" position.)

In this technique, the down lineman lines up directly over the blocker or some part of the blocker. He assumes a stance either with his feet parallel or with his inside foot slightly staggered back. Upon movement by the blocker, the defender steps into the blocker with his inside or staggered foot first. He places his head toward the blocker's inside shoulder. He puts both hands aggressively upward and into the chest of the blocker and determines the direction of the ballcarrier. If a double-team block comes, the defender drops and immediately fights pressure to prevent movement. If the blocker pulls, the defender attacks the first blocker in the direction of puller. If the blocker goes down across defender's face, he closes tight off the blocker's butt and sets for a trap. (Refer

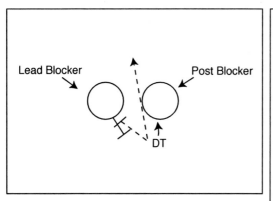

Diagram 3.7. Tech VIII vs. "double team".

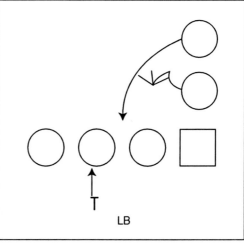

Diagram 3.9. Tech VIII vs. "option drive".

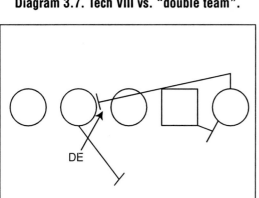

Diagram 3.8. Tech VIII vs. "trap play".

to Diagrams 3.7- 3.9)

When executing the aforementioned "eight basic techniques" in a game, the defender should engage in the following steps (in the order listed):

- Move on movement and execute the technique to the best of his ability.
- Locate the direction of the point-of-attack, and pursue relentlessly.
- Make the tackle or assist in making the tackle.

ESSENTIAL TRAITS OF A GOOD PASS RUSHER:

- Stance — close the stance similar to a sprinter's stance.
- Squeeze the line-of-scrimmage.
- Alignment — take a position that best facilitates the technique he

plans to employ (e.g. head-on, inside, or outside).

- Know where the quarterback will set-up:
    - ❏ Drop back three-to-four steps (quick passes, slants, spots, short outs, bump and run, and flys).
    - ❏ Drop back five-to-seven steps (outs, posts, and curls).
    - ❏ Drop back seven-to-nine steps (flys, out and ups, flags, and screens).
    - ❏ Sprint-out short (grain cutters, hooks, curls, flares, throw backs, short outs, and backside short posts).
    - ❏ Sprint-out long (grain cutters, flys, backside deep posts, deep outs, and comebacks).
- Study and know the type of blockers he will face:
    - ❏ Rider – rides him around the quarterback:
        - ✓ Pop and recoil.
        - ✓ Pop and stick.
    - ❏ Inside rider – invites him inside to run him into a pile-up:
        - ✓ Set and cut.
- Study and know the offensive sets and what to expect from each set.
- Do not let the blocker stick him in the chest.
- Do not go through middle of block unless he "bull rushes"; work one-half of the blocker.
- Do something to get the blocker off balance:
    - ❏ Blast him.
    - ❏ Fake him.
    - ❏ Grab and throw.
    - ❏ Out move him.

CHAPTER 4

LINEBACKERS

There are no outstanding defenses without outstanding linebackers. Linebackers who can hit and defend passes are the "heart" of a defensive unit. Technically, they are the second line of defense (down linemen being the first line). Not surprisingly if ballcarriers get past the linebackers, they generally pick up significant yardage. Likewise, when linebackers break down on pass defense, the yards gained are substantial.

DEFENDING AGAINST THE RUN

In run defense, linebackers are expected to "stuff" any hole created in the line in front of them. In order to accomplish this task, they must be good at "blocker control", intelligent enough to "read' their keys, and quick enough to get to the point-of-attack in time to make the tackle or assist in making the tackle.

Blocker Control

The linebacker must be in position to take-on blockers at all times, since he usually has to wade through blockers on his way to the ballcarrier. This special awareness requires constant "attention to business" (i.e., maintain his focus). The linebacker should stay in the "fundamental football position" as he confronts blockers. He should quickly execute "blocker control," shed the blocker, and move to make the tackle or assist in the tackle. The essence of linebacker run defense is controlling the blocker, shedding the blocker, and making the tackle.

Keying

Initially, the linebacker is basically looking at man-on-man blocking. This vertical-type blocking dictates his keying.

Strong Outside Linebacker:

- If the tight end blocks on linebacker or if the linebacker reads wide run, he executes the "ward-off" technique.
- If the tight end goes down across the linebacker's face, the linebacker reads off-tackle run and gets across the line-of-scrimmage, close off the butt of the tight end, and executes the "roadblock" technique.
- If play goes away, the linebacker gets to the depth of the ball and trails the play, searching everyone who comes his way.

Inside Linebackers:

- Read the "triangle". (Refer to Diagram 4.1)
- Zone keying for inside linebackers:
    - ❑ If the ball goes and the near back goes, "he goes" (shuffle fast).
    - ❑ If the ball stays and the near back goes, "he stays".
    - ❑ If the ball goes and the near back stays, "he goes" (shuffle slow).
- Gap-control keying for inside linebackers:
    - ❑ The linebacker reads the blocks to the right or left of the down linemen in front of him or nearest him.
    - ❑ Once the block is made on his "stack", he penetrates the offensive backfield, either watching for block in that direction or shuffles in that direction, ready to take-on the blocker. (Refer to Diagram 4.2)

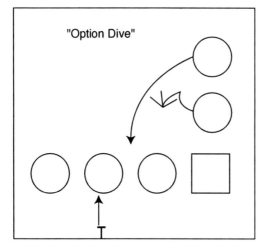

Diagram 4.1. Reading the triangle.

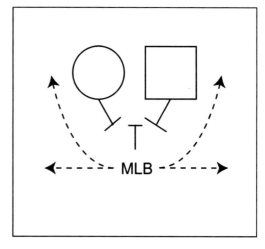

Diagram 4.2. Penetrate or shuffle.

- Guard-action keying for inside linebackers:
    - ❑ If the guard blocks down, the linebacker steps in the opposite direction, looking for a block, and takes-on the blocker with his inside shoulder and "slides" the blocker's face. (Refer to Diagram 4.3)

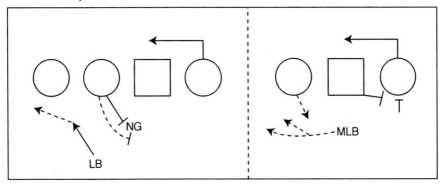

Diagram 4.3. Vs. guard down block.

    - ❑ If the guard blocks the linebacker, he steps into the blocker executing "blocker control." (Refer to Diagram 4.4)

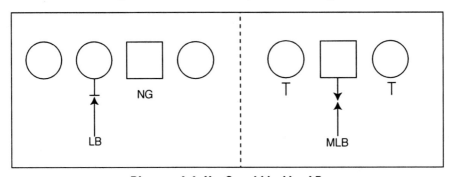

Diagram 4.4. Vs. Guard blocking LB.

    - ❑ If the guard pulls, the linebacker shuffles with him, looking for blockers and ballcarrier. (Refer to Diagram 4.5)

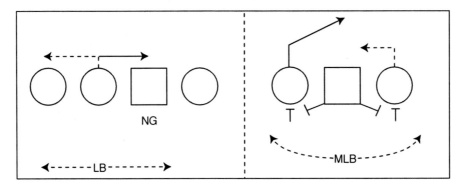

Diagram 4.5. LB vs. guard pulling.

- Option-game:
    - ❏ If the guard blocks down, the linebacker steps opposite and looks for the block.
    - ❏ If the guard takes him on, the linebacker sheds the blocker (blocker control), and makes the tackle. (Refer to Diagram 4.6)

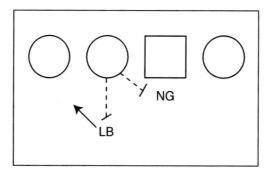

Diagram 4.6. LB vs. option.

Defensive Team – Option/Outside Run Responsibilities

In defending against wide runs, the linebacker can either out-run the offense to the point-of-attack or cut the ballcarrier off before he can "turn the corner." The latter choice is preferred. However, down linemen generally are the inside-out pursuers on wide runs. (Refer to Diagram 4.7)

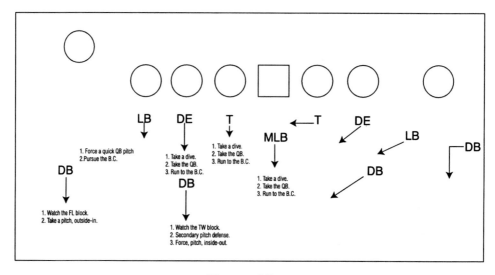

Diagram 4.7.

DEFENDING AGAINST THE PASS

On pass defense, the linebacker must be either quick enough to cover a zone or fast enough to cover a receiver man for man. When he is assigned to blitz, he must sack the quarterback or seriously hurry the quarterback because the zone/pass coverage assigned to him is now unattended. Linebackers can be aided in zone coverage by giving them "counts". The "count" system allows them the efficiency of man coverage while they are actually in zone coverage. Their "count" seldom changes. Consequently, they have the opportunity to become very good at pass coverage. The coverage procedure involves the following steps. When an "assigned receiver" starts into the linebacker's zone, the linebacker goes to him and covers him "man" until he leaves that zone, and so on, throughout the linebacker's "counts," which are seldom more than three. Simply put, the linebacker's assignments are to get into his zone quickly, and count and cover receivers in that zone. If none of the "counts" come into the zone, he should put his head on a "swivel" and continue to drop.

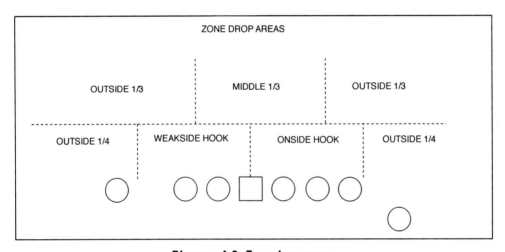

Diagram 4.8. Zone drop areas.

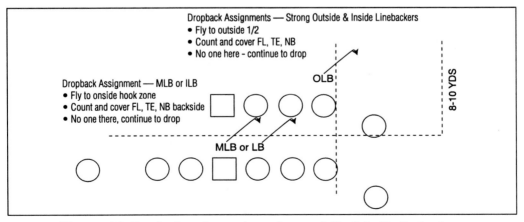

Diagram 4.9. Dropback assignments — strong outside & inside linebackers.

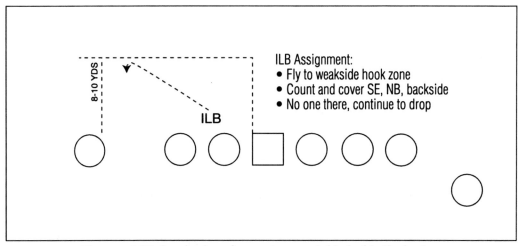

Diagram 4.10. Dropback assignment — weakside inside linebacker.

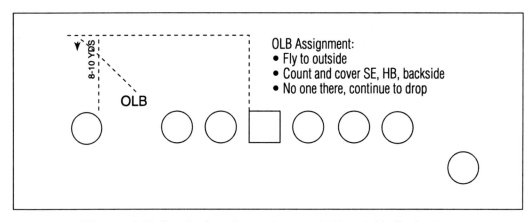

Diagram 4.11. Dropback assignment — weakside outside linebacker.

A very important teaching point is that the linebacker assignments do not change, regardless of the secondary alignment:

- Three-deep regular
- Three-deep monster
- Four-deep regular
- Twin zone
- Twin man

Sprint-out Coverage for Linebackers (Automatic Cover 3)

Whenever the ball moves beyond the offensive guard, either to the right or left, the linebacker should always move into "automatic" Cover 3. This coverage is a secondary rotation in the direction of the quarterback movement involving both man-to-man and zone principles of coverage, along with double coverage in the zones that are most vulnerable for the quarterback to attack. The linebacker assignments are identical regardless of the secondary coverage behind them. This procedure provides a great assignment advantage for the linebackers.

Containment of the Sprint-out Action

Many teams assign the last down lineman in the direction of the sprint-out as the contain-man. One of the negative features of this assignment is that it not only requires the teaching of an additional technique to the down linemen, but also requires a foot speed and agility level that few down linemen possess. Since the outside linebacker is the contain-man on runs, it seems logical for him to be the contain-man on sprint-out passes to his direction. Therefore, the recommendation is to tell the outside linebacker to execute a "ward-off" technique and aim to force the quarterback to pull-up and throw the ball near the offensive tackle's extended area. The goal is to have him "hurry" the quarterback and only make the tackle within the confines of containment. A quick delivery by the quarterback can be a tremendous benefit to the "coverers." Diagram 4-12 illus-

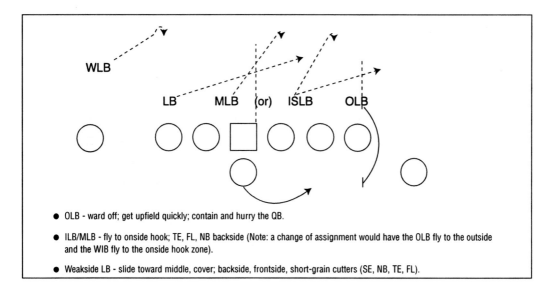

Diagram 4.12. LB assignments vs. sprint-out pass.

trates both linebacker pass drops and contain versus sprint-out pass.

Man Coverage for Linebackers

In many instances, linebackers are not as fast, nor do they have the agility of receivers. Consequently, they are at a decided mismatch when they are in a man-coverage mode. Thus, a trail technique or "hip-pocket" technique is better suited for this type of coverage. The "hip-pocket" technique offers at least two advantages: the passer is forced to be more accurate in passing to a receiver who is covered by a "hip-pocket" defender; and "hip-pocket" defenders generally have help "on the top" by a deep defender. The hip-pocket technique requires the defender to take an inside-pocket position. This position forces the passer to throw over the linebacker.

BLITZING LINEBACKERS

A linebacker should be aware of several factors that will help ensure greater success when blitzing:

- Once he starts his blitzing move, he must be relentless in his determination to get the quarterback.
- He should be well-informed as to who will block him.
- He should defeat any blockers assigned to him.
- He should time his blitz movement— whether it is at the snap of the ball or a delayed blitz.
- He should realize that when he blitzes, he leaves his normal pass-coverage area unattended, thereby adding to the urgency of his getting to the quarterback.

In many football programs, a practice exists that involves having linebacker blitzing primarily attached to man coverage in the secondary. However, it is important to remember that linebacker blitzing, regardless of necessity of the coverage behind it, should always have the same focal emphasis for the linebacker. He leaves an area unprotected, thereby highlighting the importance of the blitzers getting to the passer. The pressure is on the quarterback if the linebackers blitz, regardless if the coverage is man or zone. In this regard, the primary consideration is that most passers have generally become accustomed to linebackers blitzing only on man coverage, not on zone coverage.

CHAPTER 5

DEFENSIVE BACKS

Many football teams, regardless of the level of play (e.g., youth football, high school football, college football, or professional football), depend a great deal on their passing attack. Several years ago it was common for offenses to have a "pet" running play which they used for medium-to-long yardage situations. Currently, this "pet-play", for numerous teams, is a pass play. Not surprisingly, when a team's run offense is sputtering or a team is behind in the game, that team generally switches to its passing attack. The resulting emphasis on the forward pass has placed extreme pressure on the defensive secondary. In addition, the variety of offensive alignments that teams employ in their various attack schemes is forcing defensive backs into more one-on-one coverage situations. As a result, the margin of error for defensive backs is greatly reduced. Furthermore, a definite trend exists toward offenses using more four and five men-out pass patterns. These patterns are designed to force the classic mismatch of a fast receiver being defended by a slower linebacker or defensive back. To further worsen an already difficult situation, coaches often place their most talented and skilled athletes on offense. In order for the defense to adequately counter this situation, they should use athletes on defense with skill and talent commensurate to those who play on offense. In other words they must play skilled athletes on defense, as well as on offense.

Many coaches agree that defensive backs are among the most "skilled positions" in football. As a rule, most coaches believe that the other skilled positions include quarterbacks, running backs, and wide receivers on offense. Unfortunately, however, skilled position players not only are generally few and far between (in lieu of the necessary God-given gifts that they must possess), but they also require the greatest amount of time to train.

The late, great Paul "Bear" Bryant once said in a clinic speech in Tallahassee, Florida, "you can expect to lose one game for every freshman in your starting lineup". That statement certainly has merit when considering defensive backs. A defensive back must remember a lot of information and master a number of demanding skills before becoming a competent defender.

On the other hand the learning curve for defensive backs can be shortened several months by placing the most talented performers in the secondary positions. However, developing competency at this position still requires a considerable amount of training time. A list of the essential skills and techniques for defensive backs includes: blocker control and tackling for the run game; and back peddling, cushioning, agility, and speed for the passing game.

DEFENDING THE RUN

Blocker Control

On inside runs, the defensive back must defeat the blocks of wide receivers and offside linemen. In both of these situations, he should first try to defeat the block by using agility, quickness, movement, and anticipation rather than taking-on the blockers. However, when it becomes necessary to take-on the blocker, he should work to keep the blocker away from his body and legs.

On wide runs, similar to inside runs, the defensive back must again contend with the blocks of wide receivers, running backs, and off-side linemen. He also must be aware of a new threat to him—pulling linemen who are lead blockers for the ballcarrier. Wide runs often require the defensive back to come-up and "force" the play. He also might have to take-on blockers. One of the best ways to do this is for him to quickly get up to the line-of-scrimmage and squeeze the running lane. Then, he should take-on the blocker by going into the blocker's legs, low and hard, in order to strip the ballcarrier of blockers, thereby sacrificing his body to allow another defensive player to make the tackle. (Refer to Diagram 5.1)

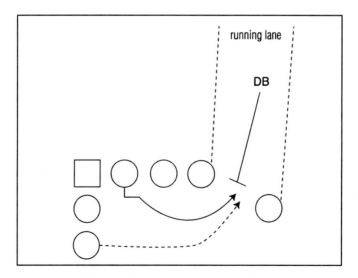

Diagram 5.1. Defending the wide run.

The defensive back cannot be the primary "force man" on wide runs if he is assigned to cover a receiver. At best, he can be expected to serve as the secondary "force man", generally forcing from outside-in. (Refer to Diagram 5.2)

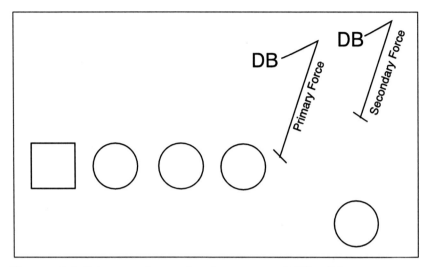

Diagram 5.2. Primary and secondary force responsibilities if in man coverage.

Tackling

Whatever assignments a coach has for his defensive backs, he should develop and have his athletes perform a drill that addresses the essential skills and techniques involved in each particular assignment and attach a tackling drill to the end of the drill.

Option Support

The following diagrams illustrate outside run and "option support" from Twins (Diagram 5.3), four-deep (Diagram 5.4), and three-deep (Diagrams 5.5-5.8) secondary alignments.

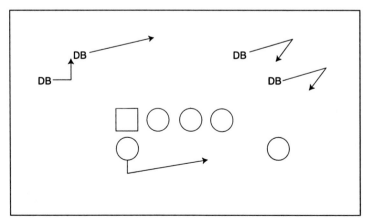

Diagram 5.3. Twins-option support strong if in zone coverage.

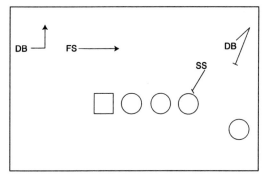

Diagram 5.4. Four-deep option support.

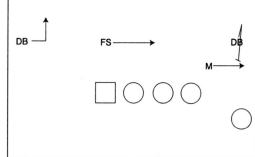

Diagram 5.5. Three-deep monster — option support strong.

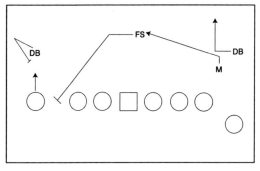

Diagram 5.6. Three-deep monster — option support weak.

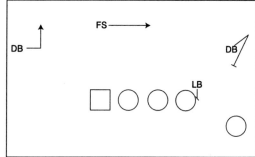

Diagram 5.7. Three-deep — option support strong.

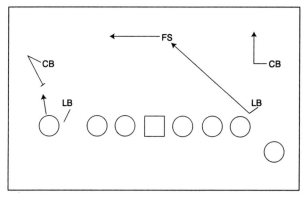

Diagram 5.8. Three-deep monster — option support weak.

Playing Down and Distance

Defensive backs aligned on wide receivers, including the free safeties and twin safeties, must always play pass first and run second regardless of the down and distance. On the other hand, the defensive backs who have primary force responsibilities should play run first and pass second. As the opponent approaches the "red zone" (i.e., the 20-yard line to the goal line), the defensive backs aligned on wide receivers, including the free safeties and twin safeties, should "squeeze" a yard or two closer in their alignments and continue this procedure on each series or each down as the opponent nears the goal line.

Regular Keys

Defensive backs aligned on wide receivers should focus on the receiver as he takes his first few strides, then pick-up quarterback movement, and then focus back to the receiver. Safeties should key the "triangle" (i.e., through the guards and the quarterback to the fullback), and locate the direction of the ball and eventually the ballcarrier. If a defensive back is in a zone coverage scheme, he should focus on the "triangle" in order to locate the ball and to determine if the play is a run or a pass. Free safeties and twin safeties should focus on the "triangle" just as the aforementioned defensive backs should do when they're in zone coverage.

DEFENDING THE PASS

Defending the pass involves several fundamentals and techniques, including back peddling, cushioning, and masking coverages.

Back Peddling

A decreasing number of coaches are teaching the back peddle because it requires extensive drilling and constant work on body position and feet movement. Instead, many coaches substitute shuffling backward in place of back peddling. When comparing good back peddlers to good back shufflers, the good back peddler has the advantage of being able to turn his hips quicker to cover the post, out, and fly patterns.

Good back-peddling body position requires the defender's hips and upper torso to be forward of his ankle joints. The defender should reach for distance in his backward step. His arms should swing vigorously to help in backward movement. Difficulty occurs when the "body lean" becomes either too straight (vertical) or a backward angle (leaning backward). As long as his body position is forward and his focus is on the receiver's lace-of-the-pants, the defender will have the body balance and anticipation in order to react to the receiver in sufficient time to cover him.

Cushioning

The appropriate level of "cushion" is usually about a yard or two distance between the defender and the receiver. The "cushion" should be maintained until the defender makes his play on the ball. Defenders get into trouble when they allow their "cushion" to be "broken" or invaded by receivers. (Refer to Diagram 5.9)

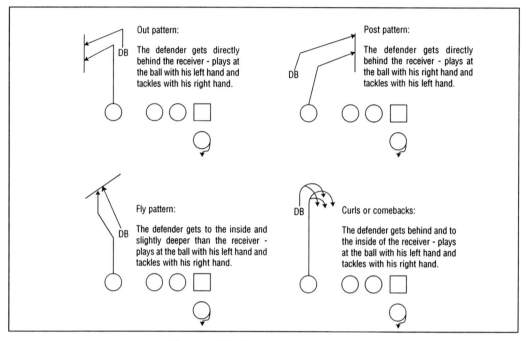

Diagram 5.9. Cushioning receivers.

Masking Coverages

The "masking" or camouflaging of secondary coverage is a counter-strategy. This innovation is the counter to the "read" patterns of the offense and involves movements by the defensive secondary that mislead the passer and receivers into thinking the coverage is something it is not. Actually, the defensive secondary is attempting to lure the passer and the receivers into a trap. Since the offensive passing game has learned to accurately read defensive secondary movements, they (the offense) can determine whether the coverage is zone, man-to-man, or a combination of both, and also who is covering whom. Therefore, it is strategically sound to utilize this knowledge to the advantage of the defensive secondary. As a result, the concept of "masking" has evolved.

Why mask coverage?

Many of the most significant innovations in football, during recent years, have occurred in the passing game. In fact, more games are being won because of strong passing attacks than because of strong running attacks. Apparently, passing skills and receiving skills are being improved at a faster pace than are secondary-coverage skills. Offenses "read" the movements and maneuvers of secondary defenders and determine, in advance, exactly how the defenses plan to cover. Contrastingly, pass defenders do not have the advantage of knowing ahead of time where the receivers are going.

From a defensive standpoint, something had to be done to head-off the rising completion rates and percentages. As a result, the masking of coverage was designed to help prevent the quarterback and receivers from reading or identifying the coverage too quickly. When the quarterback is forced to delay his delivery or look for the number two target (reset), it increases the possibilities that the pass rush will be successful.

Furthermore, when the receiver is temporarily confused or delayed in his identification of coverage, it will present problems involving delivery timing for the passer and proper route running for the receivers. For example, masking coverage tends to prohibit the passer from releasing the ball early by anticipating his receiver's moves. Thus, pass rushers are afforded more time to get to the passer. Any maneuver that aids the rushers in getting to the passer automatically makes it possible for the entire defense to play better down-and-distance football. If the passer is not sure of where his receivers will be or at what point in time they will arrive at their pre-determined area, the defender's opportunities for interceptions are greatly enhanced. Heretofore, only the hard rush, errant throw, or good defensive play caused a turnover. At this time, however, masking of secondary the coverage adds a new dimension to defensive play.

Ways to mask coverage

The most effective way to mask coverage is by alignment. In using the alignment-approach to masking coverage, the defender stations himself in an initial position that is obviously vulnerable. The intent in this instance is to mislead or bait the receiver and the quarterback, at the time of their pre-read, into attacking this obviously vulnerable alignment. However, on the snap of the ball, the defender then maneuvers to a position that removes his vulnerability and transfers it into his position of strength. The following list illustrates several options for masking.

- Inside alignment: (This is the easiest to use and to remember.) Use to the wide side of the field; use on receivers who run good out patterns (Refer to Diagram 5.10); use to the short side of the field to bait receivers into sideline patterns (Refer to Diagram 5.11); reverse this procedure for outside alignment (Refer to Diagrams 5.12 and 5.13).
- Bump-and-run, then zone: Use to the wide side of the field to force the receivers yet further away from the passer; use to get short and deep coverage on the offense's best receivers (Refer to Diagram 5.14).
- Shallow or deep: Use to confuse the receivers and the passer as to the pre-read possibilities (Refer to Diagram 5.15).
- Stack: Use to confuse the receivers and the passer as to the pre-read possibilities (Refer to Diagram 5.16).
- Four-across the board: Use to make all coverages initially appear to be one, and then rotate, move-up, move back, and move into monster or other types of coverages after the quarterback pre-reads (Refer to Diagram 5.17).
- Move zone: Cover man and visa-versa (note: zone-coverage drops involve more slants and angles, while man-coverage drops are more directly backward (Refer to Diagrams 5.18 and 5.19).
- Wave movement: Use to confuse the receiver and the passer as to the actual coverage; use to bait the passer into throwing to the strength of the coverage (Refer to Diagram 5.20).

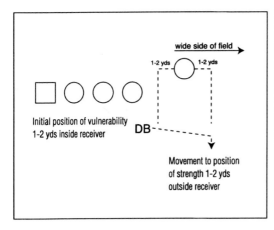

Diagram 5.10. Inside alignment to wideside receiver.

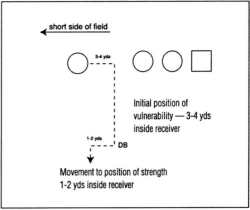

Diagram 5.11. Inside alignment to shortside receiver.

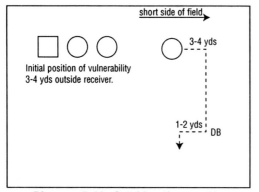

Diagram 5.12. Outside alignment to shortside receiver.

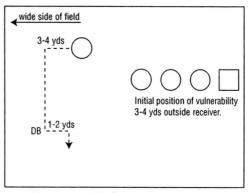

Diagram 5.13. Outside alignment to wideside receiver.

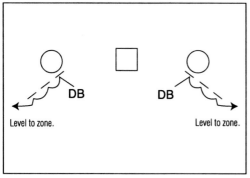

Diagram 5.14. Bump-and-run adjustment.

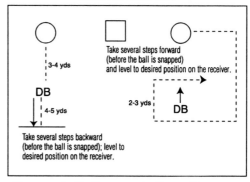

Diagram 5.15. Deep or shallow adjustment.

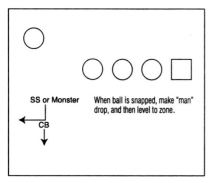

Diagram 5.16. Stack adjustment.

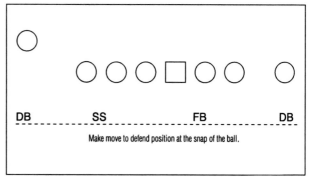

Diagram 5.17. Four-across adjustment.

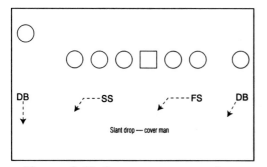

Diagram 5.18. Four-across — zone deep.

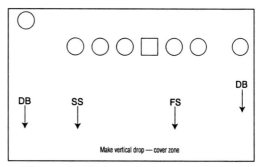

Diagram 5.19. Four-across — man drops.

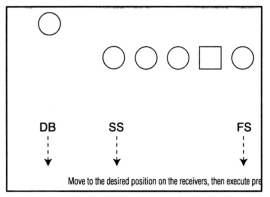

Diagram 5.20. Wave movement.

Defensive Back Drills

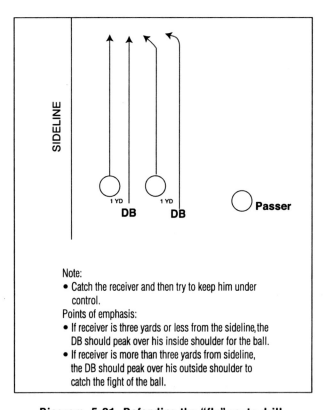

Diagram 5.21. Defending the "fly" route drill.

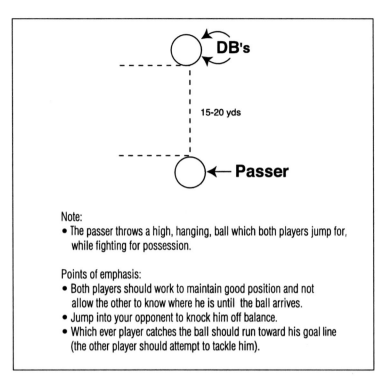

Diagram 5.22. Jump and fight drill.

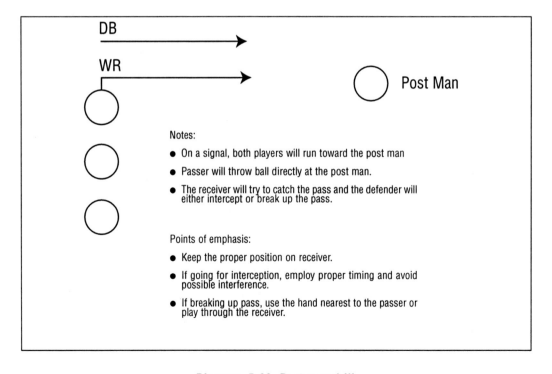

Diagram 5.23. Post man drill.

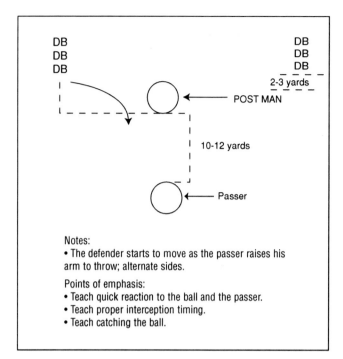

Diagram 5.24. Take it drill.

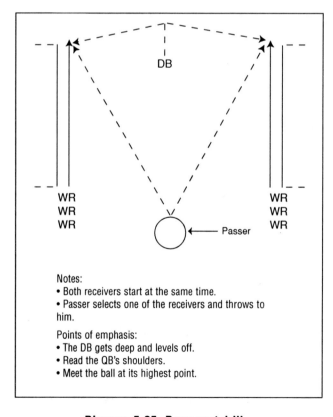

Diagram 5.25. Deep post drill.

Pass Defense Zones

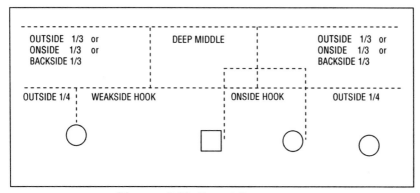

Diagram 5.26. Pass defense zones.

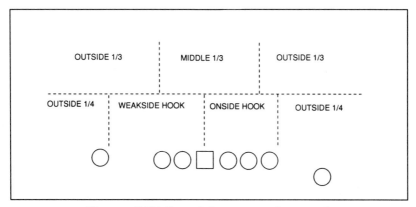

Diagram 5.27. Pass defense zones for cover 3.

Zone Coverages on Dropback Passes

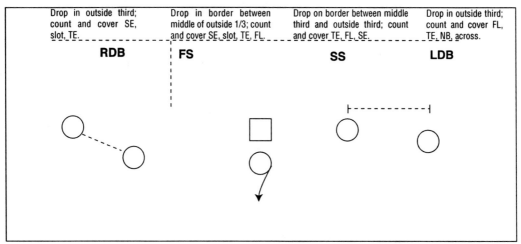

Diagram 5.28. Dropback — four-deep — all out zone.

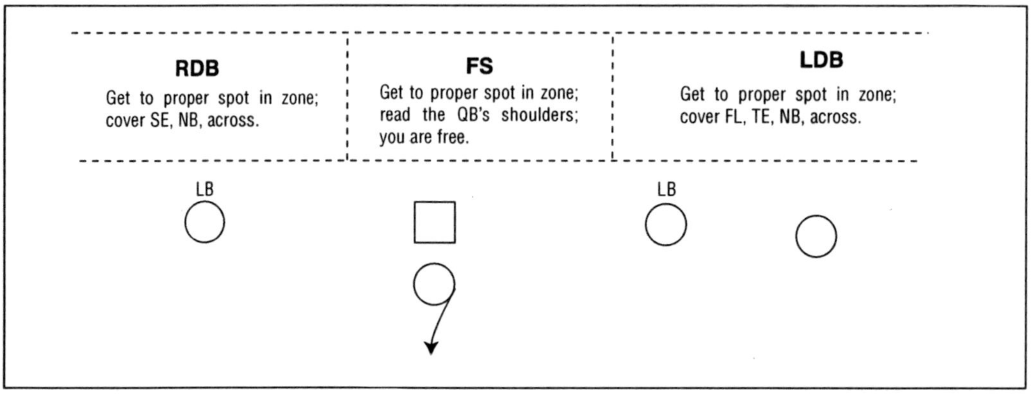

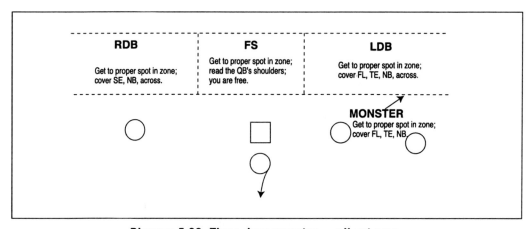

Diagram 5.29. Dropback — three-deep — all out zone.

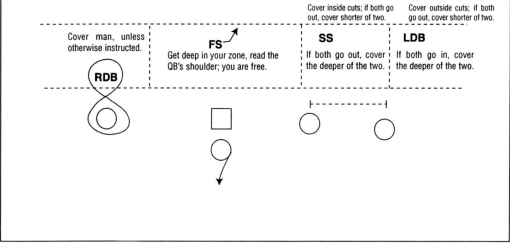

Diagram 5.30. Three-deep monster — all out zone.

Diagram 5.31. Four-deep dropback — Cover I zone and man.

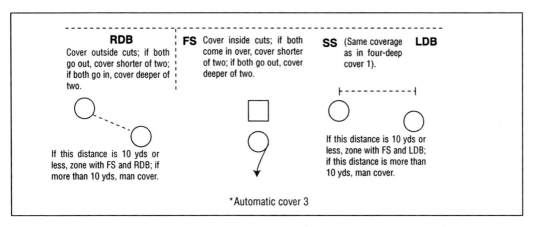

Diagram 5.32. Four-deep dropback to double formation — Cover I zone and man.

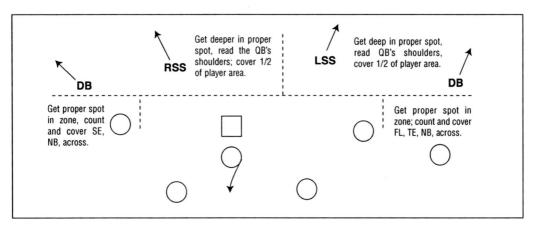

Diagram 5.33. Dropback twins — all out zone.

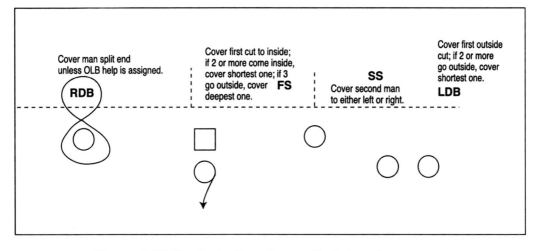

Diagram 5.34. Dropback - Three to one side (automatic coverage).

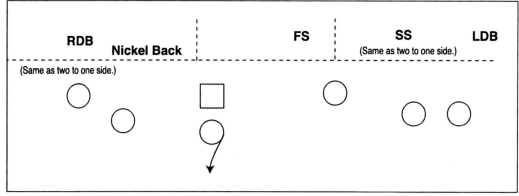

Diagram 5.35. Dropback - three to one side, two to other side (automatic).

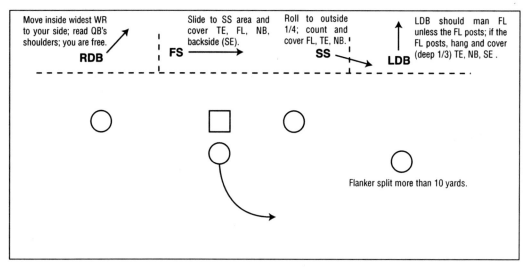

Diagram 5.36. Automatic Cover 3 — QB roll and the flanker split more than 10 yards.

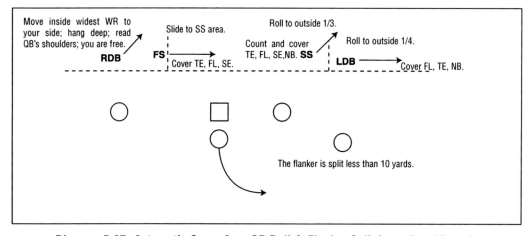

Diagram 5.37. Automatic Cover 3 — QB Roll & Flanker Split Less than 10 yards

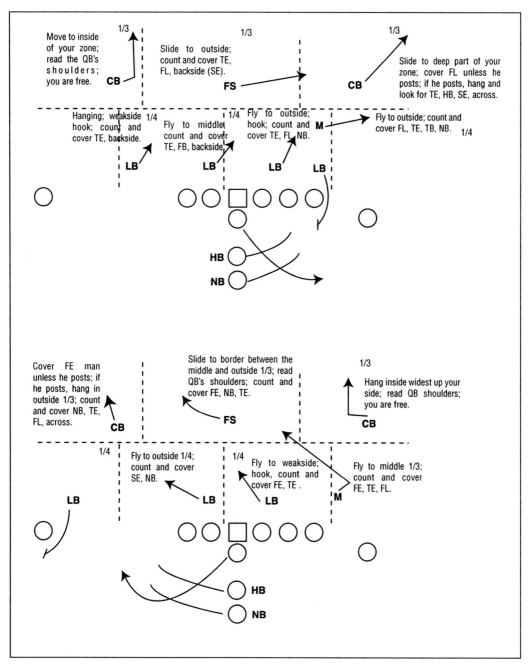

Diagram 5.38. Cover 3, 3-deep monster.

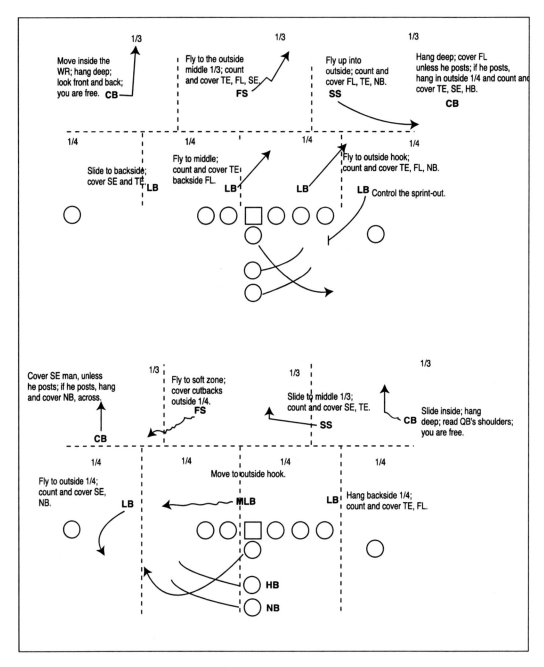

Diagram 5.39. 4-deep, zone-man coverage.

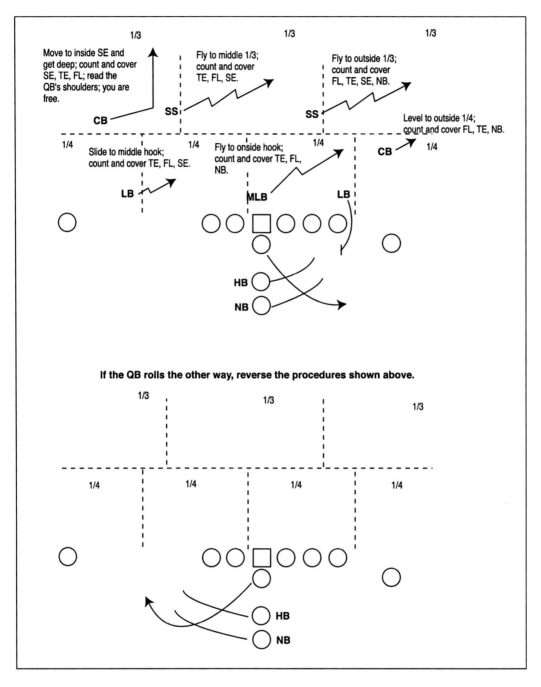

Diagram 5.40. Cover 3 — Twin.

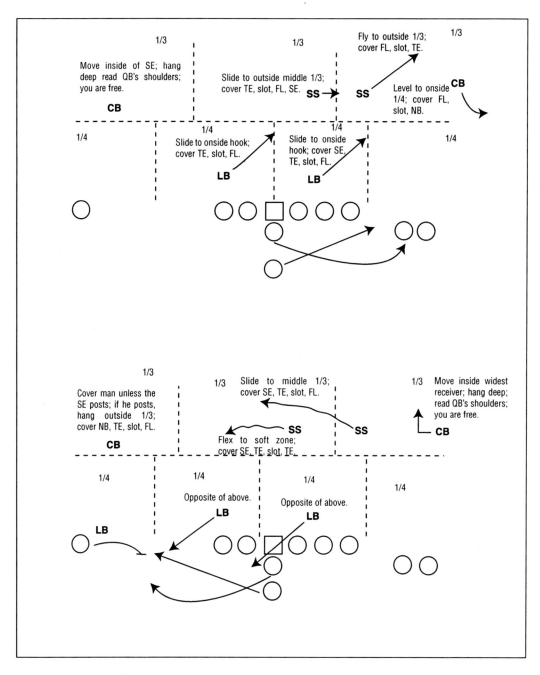

Diagram 5.41. Cover 3 with three to one side from twins.

Cover 3 Assignments versus QB Roll-Out:

Left Defensive Back (LDB)

- If the quarterback rolls to the side of the LDB and the flanker's "split" is less than 10 yards, the LDB rolls to the onside 1/4, counts, and covers flanker, tight end, and near back.
- If the quarterback rolls to the side of the LDB and the flanker's "split" is more than 10 yards, the LDB covers the flanker unless the flanker posts; if the flanker posts, the LDB hangs outside 1/3, and covers the tight end, near back, and across.
- If the quarterback rolls away, the LDB moves inside of the widest receiver to his side, hangs deep, and reads the quarterback's shoulders; the LDB is free.

Strong Safety (SS)

- If the quarterback rolls to the SS and the flanker's "split" is less than 10 yards, the SS rolls to the outside 1/3, counts, and covers the flanker, tight end, near back, and backside (across).
- If the quarterback rolls to the SS and the flanker's "split" is less than 10 yards, the SS rolls to the outside 1/3, counts, and covers the flanker, tight end, near back.
- If the quarterback rolls away from the strong safety, the SS slides to the onside of middle 1/3, counts, and covers the split end, tight end, and backside flanker.

Free Safety (FS)

- If the quarterback rolls toward the flanker, the free safety slides toward the flanker, counts, and covers the tight end, flanker, and backside (split end).
- If the quarterback rolls toward the split end, and he is split, the free safety slides toward the split end ("soft zone"), counts, and covers the split end posts backside tight end, and backside flanker.
- If the split end is tight, the free safety flys to the outside 1/3, counts, and covers the split end, the near back, the backside tight end, and then flanker.

Right Defensive Back (RDB)

- If the quarterback rolls toward the flanker, the RDB moves inside the widest receiver to his side and hangs deep, and reads the quarterback's shoulders; the RDB is free.
- If the quarterback rolls toward the split end, the RDB covers the split end "man" unless the split end posts; if he posts, the RDB hangs in the deep 1/3, counts, and covers the near back, the backside tight end, and then the flanker.

Three-Deep Regular Dropback to Automatic Cover 3 Assignments:

Left Defensive Back (LDB)

- Same as four-deep regular; cover the outside 1/3 zone.

Strong Safety (SS)

- Zone with the left-defensive-back.

Left Outside Linebacker (LOLB)

- If the quarterback rolls to the LOLB, the LOLB should ward off, get upfield, and contain quarterback.
- If the quarterback rolls away from the LOLB, the LOLB should fly to the middle 1/3, count, and cover the split end, tight end, backside, and flanker backside.

Free Safety (FS)

- Same as in four-deep regular; cover the middle 1/3 zone.

Right Defensive Back (RDB)

- Same as in four-deep regular; cover the outside 1/3 zone.

Three-Deep Monster Dropback to Automatic Cover 3 Assignments:

Left Defensive Back (LDB)

- Same as in four-deep regular; cover the outside 1/3 zone.

Monster

- Same as three-deep monster; cover the outside 1/4 zone.
- If the quarterback rolls away, the monster must fly to middle 1/3 and cover the split end on posts; and the tight end backside.

Free Safety (FS)

- Same as three-deep regular; cover the middle 1/3 zone.

Right Defensive Back (RDB)

- Same as three-deep regular: cover the outside 1/3 zone.

> **Four-Deep Dropback Cover 1 Zone and Man Coverage to Automatic Cover 3 (All Assignments Are Same as in Four-Deep Regular)**

Dropback Twins to Automatic Cover 3 Assignments:

Left Defensive Back

- If the quarterback rolls to the LDB's level in the outside 1/4, the LDB counts; and then covers the flanker, tight end, and near back
- If the quarterback rolls away from the LDB, gets deep quickly, moves on the inside of the widest receiver, and reads the quarterback's shoulders; the LDB is free

Left Safety

- If the quarterback rolls to the LS, the LS flys to the outside 1/3, counts, and then covers the flanker, tight end, and backside.
- If the quarterback rolls away, the LS slides to the middle 1/3, counts, and then covers the split end, tight end, backside, and flanker backside.

Right Safety (RS)

- If the quarterback rolls away, the RS slides to the middle 1/3, counts, and then covers the tight end, flanker, and backside split end
- If the quarterback rolls to the side of the RS, the RS flys to the outside 1/3, counts, and then covers the split end, and tight end backside.

Right Defensive Back (RDB)

- If the quarterback rolls away, the RDB moves to the inside of the widest receiver, gets deep quickly; and reads the quarterback's shoulders; the RDB is free.
- If the quarterback rolls to the side of the RCB, the RCB levels into the outside 1/4, counts, and then covers the split end, and near back.

Dropback – Three to One Side to Automatic Cover 3 Assignments:

Left Defensive Back (LDB)

- If the split end is tight and the quarterback rolls to the LDB, rotate up into outside 1/4; count, and cover the flanker, tight end, near back.
- If the split end is split, cover him "man" unless he posts.
- If the split end posts, hang in outside 1/3, count, and cover the tight end, near back, and flanker.
- If the quarterback rolls away, move inside the widest receiver to his side, hang deep, read the quarterback's shoulders, the LDB is free.

Middle Defensive Back (MDB)

- If the quarterback rolls away from the MDB should and the split end is tight, the MDB fly to outside 1/3, count, and cover the split end, tight end backside, and flanker backside.
- If the split end is split, level to "soft zone", count, and cover the split end, tight end, backside, and flanker backside.

Right Defensive Back (RDB)

- If the quarterback rolls away from the RDB, move inside and deep of the widest receiver to his side; read the quarterback's shoulders; the RDB is free.
- If the quarterback rolls to the side of the RDB, and the split end is tight, rotate up into the outside 1/4, count, and cover the split end, near back, and across.
- If the quarterback rolls to the RDB and the split end is split, cover him "man" unless he posts; if he posts, hang in outside 1/3, count and cover near back, tight end backside, and flanker backside.

Dropback Three to One Side, Two to the Other Side Assignments:

Left Defensive Back, Middle Defensive Back, Free Safety

- Same assignment as on the "three to one side"; zone the "three to one side"

Nickel Back (NB)

- If the quarterback rolls away, the NB slides to the middle 1/3, counts and covers the tight end, middle receiver, backside slot, flanker, and backside split end.

- If the quarterback rolls to the side of the NB, and the split end is tight, the NB flys to the outside 1/3, counts and covers the split end, slot, tight end backside, and middle receiver backside.

- If the quarterback rolls to the NB, and the split end is split, the NB slides to "soft zone"; counts, and covers the split end (post), tight end back-side, and middle receiver backside.

Right Defensive Back (RDB)

- If the quarterback rolls away, the RDB moves inside and deep on the widest receiver to his side; read the quarterback's shoulders; the RDB is free.

- If the quarterback rolls to the side of the RDB, and the split end is tight, the RDB rotates up into outside 1/4, counts, and covers the split end, near back, across.

- If the quarterback rolls to the side of the RDB, and the split end is split, the RDB covers him man unless he posts; if he posts, the RDB hangs in the outside 1/3, counts, and covers the near back, tight end backside, and middle receiver backside.

Man Coverage

Man-to-man pass coverage is probably the most difficult coverage for a defensive back because it requires so many attributes that the average defensive back does not possess. A good man-cover defensive back must have football "smarts", great agility and quickness. He also must be physically strong, have outstanding foot-speed, and the mental discipline to quickly recover from adversity. The height factor is an intangible because what a shorter player gives up in the lack of height, he can often make-up for with a higher level of agility and quickness because of his lower center of gravity. Among the essential attributes of successful man coverage are the following:

- Take away two. This precept originates from a wide receiver's "basic cuts"— fly, out, and in. All other receiver's cuts come off these three "basics". As the defensive back starts his back peddle, he should adhere to certain principles and guidelines. For example, he must maintain his cushion at all times. Furthermore, he must always take away the receiver's "fly" option first in all situations. Accordingly, he should be in a position of strength for either the "out" or "in" cut, depending on where his "help" is. His "help" is either another defender who is in position to assist or the sideline stripe (out-of-bounds).

- Cushion. Stay on balance and into back peddle as long as the receiver does not break your cushion, (if he does break your cushion turn and run with back facing inside), or until he makes an out-cut or in-cut.

- Focus on the lace of the receiver's pants. As the receiver comes off the line-of-scrimmage, the defender initially glances at him, then looks quickly at the quarterback (to establish that he is still in man coverage), and finally focuses on the lace of the receiver's pants (the slowest moving spot on the receiver). When the lace drops, the defensive back should get ready to quickly react to either an "in" cut or an "out" cut.

- Position on receiver. The defensive back should work to maintain the one-to-two yard distance and the proper position on the receiver.

- Playing the ball. If the defensive back must play "through" the receiver to get to the ball, he should "time" his arrival to the ball (so as not to interfere with the receiver's opportunity to catch the pass), and play hard, using both hands to thrust swiftly downward. If the receiver is going to the right or left ("in cut or out cut"), the defensive back should play the ball with the hand nearest to the passer and be ready to tackle the receiver with the other hand if the receiver catches the ball.

- Emotion. Defensive backs should work hard to maintain an "even keel", not too high when they are doing well, and not too low when they are not doing well. Such a level of emotional control will better allow them to stay in the game mentally. Without question, "man" coverage is one of the most difficult assignments in football, almost as difficult as it is to complete passes against "man" coverage.

- The "bump and run". When bump-and-run coverage was first introduced, the rules allowed the defensive back to bump the receiver until the ball was in the air. On the process, the rules provided the defenders with a decided advantage over the receiver. As a result, pass offenses suffered. In recent years, the rules have been turning back in favor of the receivers. For example, one major adjustment in the rules mandates that a receiver cannot be touched after he has gone five yards beyond the LOS until the defender makes a play on the ball. The current rules concerning contact between the receiver and the defender are designed to curtail the defender from harassing and knocking the receiver off his route. As a consequence, while the "bump and run" is still a weapon, it is not as formidable as it once was.

- Blitzing: Any defender within five-to-seven yards of the line-of-scrimmage is counted as a defender against the run and as a possible blitzer against the pass. Offenses are often in a quandary as to what these "in between" defenders are going to do. Defenses, on the other hand, are constantly trying to camouflage these "in between" defenders so that they appear to be what they're not. One way to do this is to have a defensive back "time" his movement toward the line-of-scrimmage so that he catches the quarterback at a time when he can no longer audible the play. Another possible option for a defensive back is to "sneak" up into the area from which he can blitz. A third alternative occurs when offenses fail to adequately split their receivers wide enough. As a result, a defender is aligned nearer his blitzing point and cannot be accounted for by other protectors.

CHAPTER 6

TAKE AWAY THE RUN FIRST

MAKE THE OFFENSE "ONE DIMENSIONAL"

All other factors being equal, the defense is being "out hit" if the offense is consistently successful at running the football. Therefore, if the defense plans to take away the run, it becomes paramount for it to hit hard, tackle aggressively, run fast, and do a superior job at "blocker control". If the defense effectively shuts down the run, it renders the opponent's offense "one dimensional". In the process, it forces the offense to pass in order to move the football. When this happens, the defense can use alignments and personnel that are stronger against the pass because the run is no longer a realistic option for its opponent.

Power plays, inside isolations, traps, and option dives that are blocked well are normally difficult, but not impossible to stop. If the "one dimension" becomes the run, the opponent is in control of the game because he now controls both the ball and the clock. Accordingly, the running game presents a clear and present challenge to the defense.

Good running teams are usually especially strong at running off tackle. This factor tends to re-enforce the often- repeated football coach's adage: "the tackle hole" is a "hitter's hole." In fact, whichever team, the offense or the defense, controls the "tackle hole" controls the running game. The logic behind such a statement lies in the fact that by the time offensive and defensive players reach the tackle hole, their velocity is relatively high, thereby often resulting in tremendous collisions, i.e., "a hitter's hole".

Many teams try to get "outside" by using the option. Solid assignments, discipline, and the willingness to get to the point-of-attack tend to be very effective tools against the option. Not surprisingly, teams that have outstanding speed in the backfield force defensive teams to run hard to arrive at the point-of-attack in time to stop wide runs.

DEFENDING REVERSES AND MISDIRECTION

Reverses tend to work best against defenses whose players do not carry out their assignments exactly as specified. Naked reverses (i.e., reverses without blockers) only work when assignment breakdowns occur with perimeter players. Outside linebackers and defensive ends should be taught to "search" all players that come toward them (quarterbacks, running backs, wide receivers), and get to the depth of the ball when trailing plays. The secondary player assigned to "hang" on the backside should do exactly that while he thoroughly "searches" all offensive players coming toward him.

In defending "misdirection" plays, discipline is the most important factor. All players on the defense should have "keys" (i.e., offensive players whose movement tells the defense the point-of-attack). Defensive coaches must establish and teach players their "keys" and what those keys mean. It is also advisable to practice team defense without facing offensive backs for the first few days against a misdirection team. (Refer to Diagrams 6.1 and 6.2)

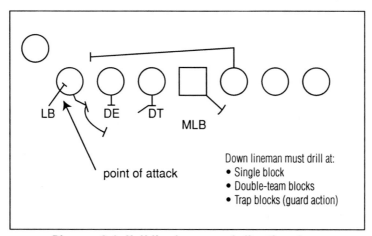

Diagram 6.1. Half-line keys vs. misdirection plays.

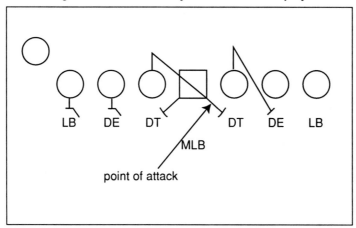

Diagram 6.2. 7-on-7 keys vs. misdirection plays.

Down Linemen and Linebacker "Keys":

- Defensive tackle (DT). Read the head of offensive guard; if he pulls, attack the center and run to football.
- Defensive end (DE). If tight end is tight, watch the offensive tackle; if tight end is not there, read the head of the tackle. Block and run to the football.
- Outside linebacker (OLB). Step into tight end, if he goes down inside, close off his butt and look for inside out block. If he blocks on the OLB, read his head.
- Middle linebacker (MLB). Read the "triangle", and go with the pullers; watch the block from the linemen.

The Box

"The number in the box" is a football term that is used to identify the number of defensive players aligned in the area extending laterally from the tight end on one side to a few yards beyond the tackle on the other side, and vertically from the line of scrimmage to four-or-five yards deep. This area can include down linemen, linebackers, and defensive backs. (Refer to Diagram 6.3)

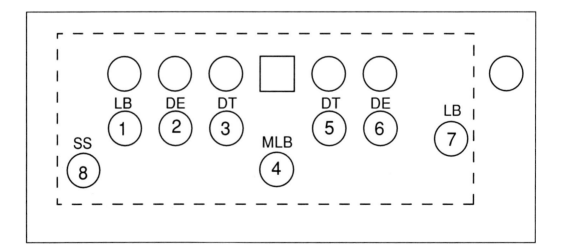

Diagram 6.3. The box.

The fewer players needed in the "box" to take away the run, the greater the probability of having an outstanding defense. Once the defense forces the offense into predictable situations, the defense is more likely to stay ahead of the offense. When this situation occurs, the defense is in a very positive position.

Many quarterbacks are taught their audible system by using the number of defensive players in the box to determine whether the play should be a run or pass. For example, if the number of defensive players in the box is less than seven, the play should be a run unless down-and-distance dictates differently. On the other hand, if the number of defensive players in the box is seven or more, the play should be a pass, unless dictated otherwise.

DOWN LINEMEN AND LINEBACKERS VERSUS BLOCKING SCHEMES

Solid game preparation and good practice organization require drilling linemen and linebackers on the techniques that they should employ to handle the various blocking schemes. This approach should also allow adequate time to be spent on seven-on-seven pass drills so the secondary will be sufficiently prepared to handle the demands that they will face in the game-situations. Defensive coaches, through film study, must decide what type of blocking schemes they are likely to face against a particular opponent and "feed" their linemen and linebackers those schemes during practice.

- *Zone blocking schemes.* This blocking scheme, generally involves each offensive blockers putting his "hat" on each defensive player, "mano-e-mano". That places the defense in a "read-the-head-of-the-blocker" and blocker-control type of defensive play. The ballcarrier picks his hole wherever there is a split in the defense. (Refer to Diagram 6.4)

- *Gap-control defense.* In playing gap-control defense, a defensive front either lines-up in gaps or stunts into gaps. The defense has to "occupy" six offensive gaps. In occupy all six gaps, the defense needs a combination of six down linemen and linebackers committed to the gaps. (Refer to Diagram 6.5)

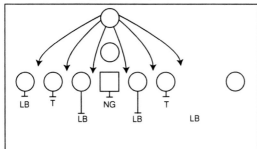

Diagram 6.4. Blocker control defense.

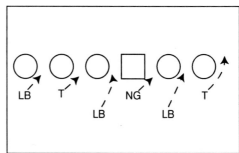

Diagram 6.5. Gap control defense.

- *Guard-action defense.* In defending against a guard-action offense, the defense must prepare to handle the following types of situations: (Refer to Diagrams 6.6 and 6.7)
    - Single blocking
    - Double-team blocking at all holes except on the split end
    - Trap blocking
    - Guard pulling, and either the tackle or tight end pulling

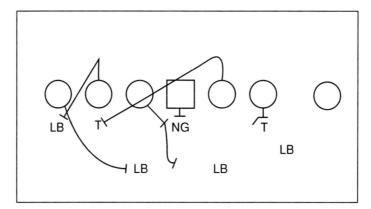

Diagram 6.6. Guard pull defense vs. inside trap.

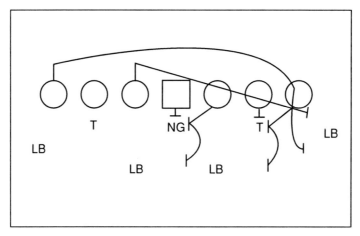

Diagram 6.7. Guard and TE pull defense vs. outside trap.

- *Option-game defense.* When defending against the option game, it is advisable to get as many people as possible to the three points-of-attack on each side of the center. (Refer to Diagram 6.8)

DEFENDING OPTION TEAMS

Against option teams, the "split" look up front is recommended because it is difficult to block on inside runs. Twins in the secondary is generally the most effective alignment because the corners can be "rolled-up" on both sides to better defend against pitches. (Refer to Diagram 6.9)

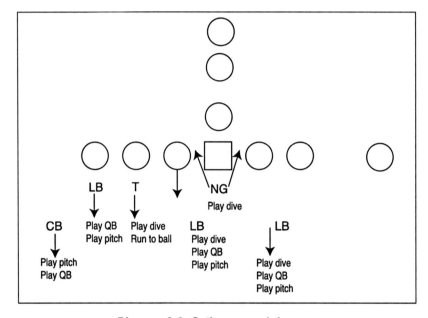

Diagram 6.8. Option-game defense.

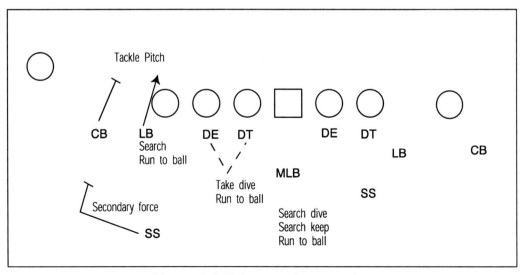

Diagram 6.9. Twins secondary vs. option.

Combining Odd Fronts and Even Fronts

It is an advantage for the defense to switch from an odd from to an even front without substitutions because of the following:

- It does not allow the offense the opportunity to substitute in an effort to counter the change of fronts.
- It does not allow the offense time to anticipate what front they will see next.
- Only two of the eleven players have assignment changes (right outside linebacker and left inside linebacker).
- The odd front right outside linebacker forces the offense to block him with a smaller back or slide the entire offensive line to match a "big-on-big" blocking situation.
- The even front right outside linebacker is matched against a slower tackle on the blind side of the quarterback in pass situations. Refer to Diagrams 6.10 and 6.11

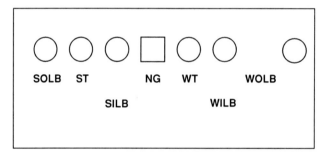

Diagram 6.10. Odd front.

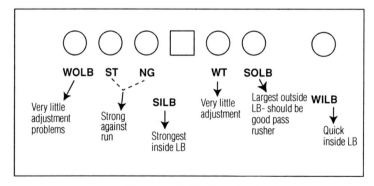

Diagram 6.11. Even front.

Secondary Adjustments to Formations, Shifts, and Motions

The word "automatic" is defined as, "without conscious thought or delay." In a football sense, "automatically" is the way secondary defenders must execute their assignments as they deal with the variety of spread formations, and potential shifts and motions from these formations. A defender might see different combinations of alignments, backfield and receiver shifts, and motion all on a single play. When secondary assignments are not "automatic", the likelihood of making an assignment error increases tremendously. However, if the secondary performs their assignments in an "automatic" fashion, the possibility that they will make an error in judgment is greatly diminished. Ultimately, pass defenders "live and die" by their ability to quickly execute their assignments in an appropriate, precise manner. Diagrams 6.12 to 6.19 illustrate several examples of the types of adjustments that the secondary must make to specific situations.

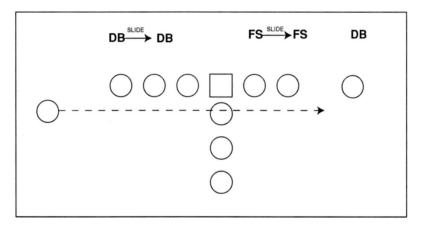

Diagram 6.12. Slide adjustment vs. flanker motion (3 deep).

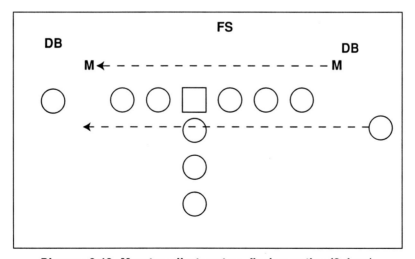

Diagram 6.13. Monster adjustment vs. flanker motion (3 deep).

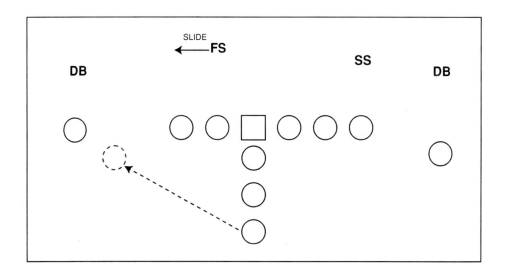

Diagram 6.14. Freesafety slide adjustment to tailback shift weak (4 deep).

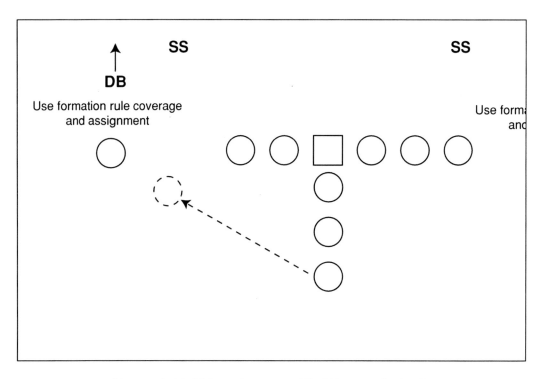

Diagram 6.15. Slide assignment to TB shift strong (4 deep).

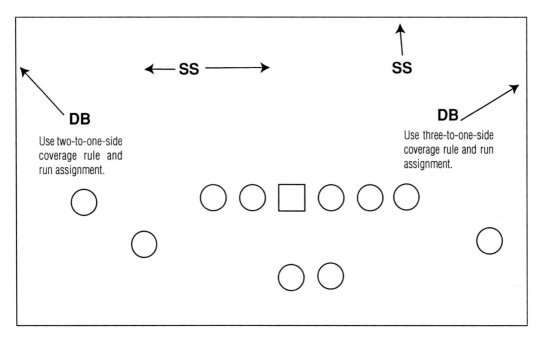

Diagram 6.16. Double formation adjustment (Twins).

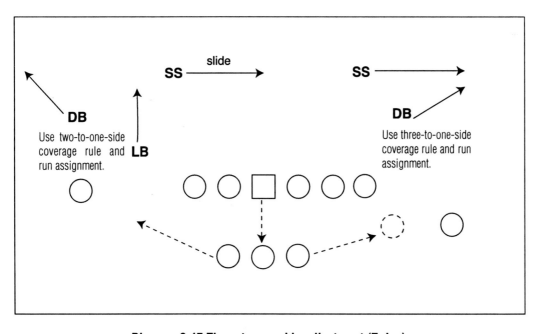

Diagram 6.17 Three-to-one side adjustment (Twins).

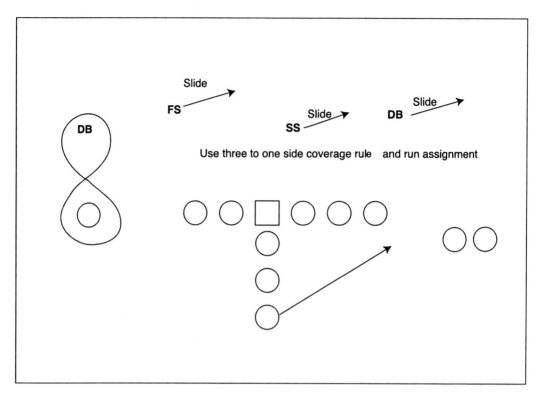

Diagram 6.18. Double formation in adjustment (Twins).

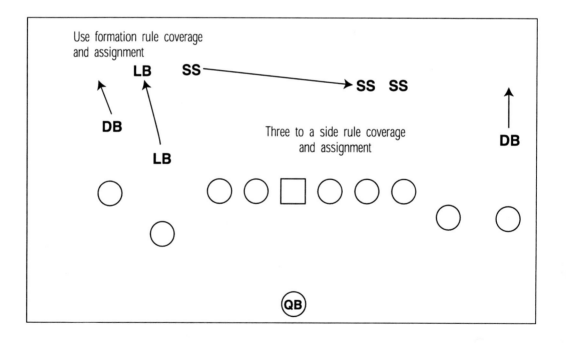

Diagram 6.19. Double formation backside adjustment (Twins).

Entire Defenses

In previous chapters the defensive line, the linebackers and the secondary have been discussed and are "units of the whole." The "entire defense" is built by using the eight basic techniques for linebackers and the secondary. The following diagrams 6.20-6.25 and assignments include all defensive positions.

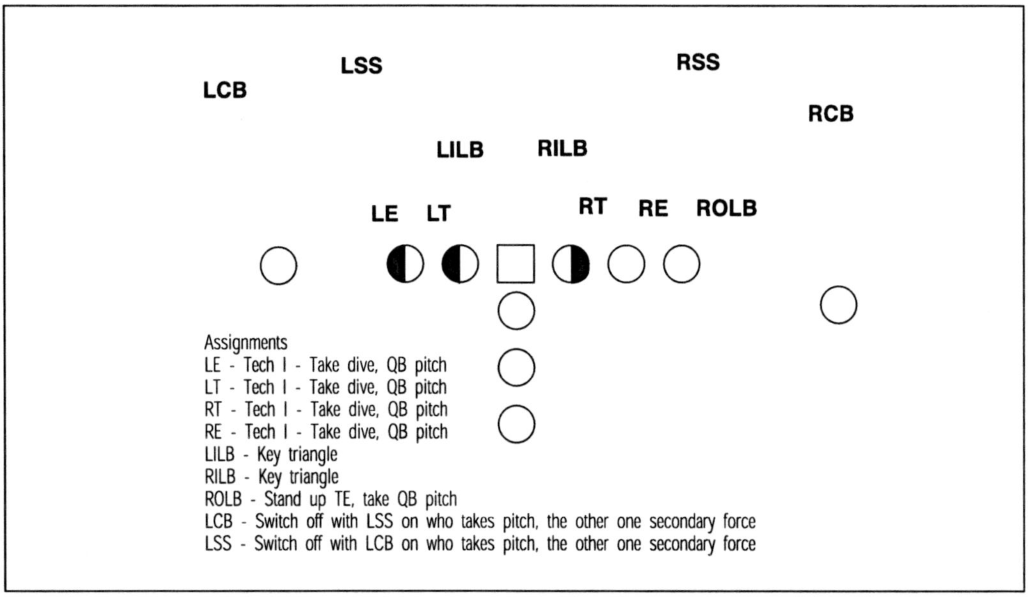
LSS
RSS
LCB
RCB
LILB
RILB
LE
LT
RT
RE
ROLB
Assignments
LE - Tech I - Take dive, QB pitch
LT - Tech I - Take dive, QB pitch
RT - Tech I - Take dive, QB pitch
RE - Tech I - Take dive, QB pitch
LILB - Key triangle
RILB - Key triangle
ROLB - Stand up TE, take QB pitch
LCB - Switch off with LSS on who takes pitch, the other one secondary force
LSS - Switch off with LCB on who takes pitch, the other one secondary force

Diagram 6.20. 40 split — Twins.

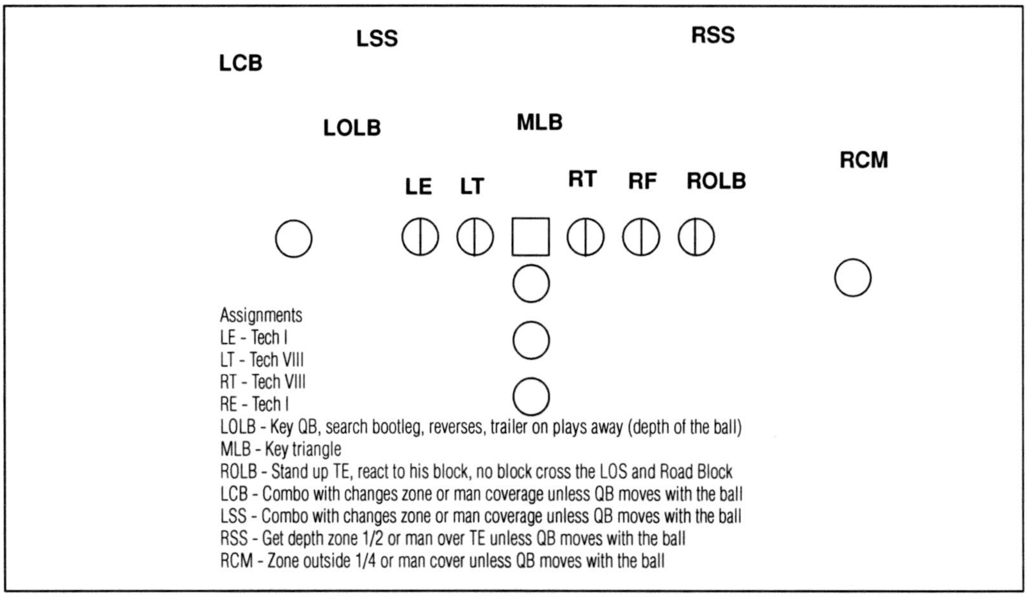
LSS
RSS
LCB
LOLB
MLB
RCM
LE
LT
RT
RF
ROLB
Assignments
LE - Tech I
LT - Tech VIII
RT - Tech VIII
RE - Tech I
LOLB - Key QB, search bootleg, reverses, trailer on plays away (depth of the ball)
MLB - Key triangle
ROLB - Stand up TE, react to his block, no block cross the LOS and Road Block
LCB - Combo with changes zone or man coverage unless QB moves with the ball
LSS - Combo with changes zone or man coverage unless QB moves with the ball
RSS - Get depth zone 1/2 or man over TE unless QB moves with the ball
RCM - Zone outside 1/4 or man cover unless QB moves with the ball

Diagram 6.21. 40 regular — Twins.

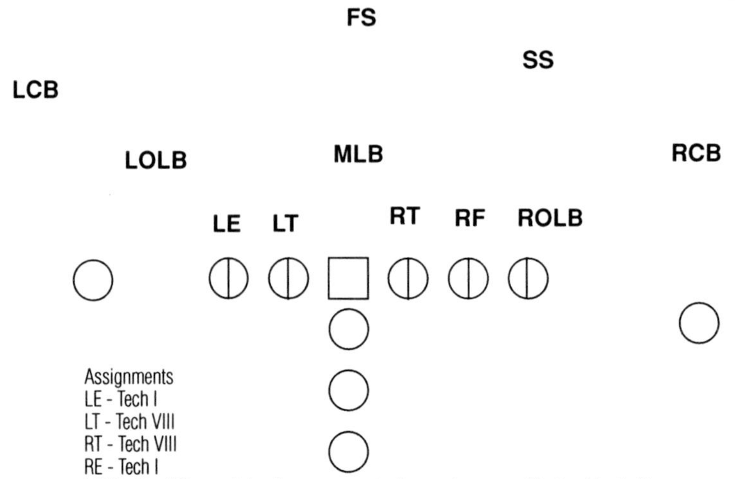

Diagram 6.22. 40 regular — 4 deep zone/man.

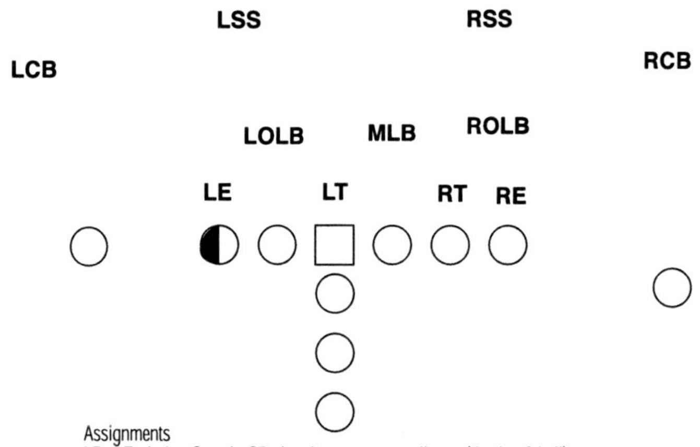

Assignments
LE - Tech I
LT - Tech VIII
RT - Tech VIII
RE - Tech I
LOLB - Key QB, search bootleg, reverses, trailer on plays away (depth of the ball)
MLB - Key triangle
ROLB - Stand up TE, react to his block, no block cross the LOS and Road Block
LCB - Man coverage on SE unless QB moves with the ball
FS - You are free
SS - Key TE through to QB, unless QB moves with the ball
RCB - Zone or man coverage, unless QB moves with the ball

Diagram 6.23. 40 over — Twins.

Assignments
LE - Tech I - Search QB, bootleg, reverse trailer - (depth of ball)
LT - Tech I or Tech IV (controlled by MLB)
RT - Tech VIII
RE - Tech I - Search QB, bootleg, reverse trailer - (depth of ball)
LOLB - Key triangle
MLB - Key triangle control LT technique
ROLB - Key through TE to QB
LCB - Combo with SS on coverage unless QB moves with the ball
LSS - Combo with LCB on coverage unless QB moves with the ball
RSS - Key through TE to QB
RCB - Man coverage on FL unless QB moves with the ball

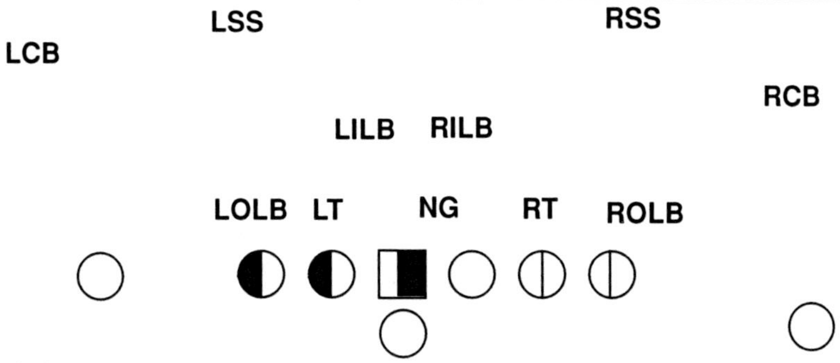

Assignments
- LE - Tech I, take dive, QB, pitch
- NG - Tech I or Tech IV (controlled by RILB) take dive, QB, pitch
- RT - Tech I, Take dive, QB, pitch
- LOLB - Tech I, take dive, QB, pitch - Trailer -depth of ball
- LILB - Key triangle, take dive, QB, pitch
- RILB - Key triangle, take dive, QB, pitch (control tech of NG)
- ROLB - Stand up TE, key through to QB, take QB, pitch
- LCB - Combo change up on pitch unless QB moves with the ball
- LSS - Combo changes up on pitch unless QB moves with the ball
- RSS - Key through TE to QB, take pitch unless QB moves with the ball
- RCB - Man coverage on FL, secondary force the pitch unless QB moves with the ball

Diagram 6.24. OKIE — over-Twins.

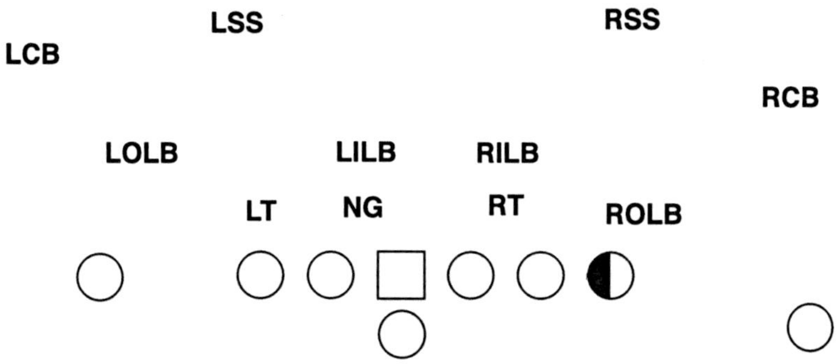

Assignments
- LE - Head up, Tech I
- NG - Tech VI, penetrate, run BC down
- RT - Tech III or IV (controlled by RILB)
- LOLB - Key QB, search bootleg, and reverses, trailer on plays away (depth of ball)
- LILB - Key block on NG, penetrate, run BC down
- RILB - Control the tech of RT, key block, penetrate, run BC down
- ROIB - Inside shoulder TE, protect stack, read TE block
- LCB - Combo - man or zone coverage unless QB moves with the ball
- LSS - Combo - man or zone coverage unless QB moves with the ball
- RSS - Key through TE to QB
- RCB - Man coverage on FL unless QB moves with the ball

Diagram 6.25. OKIE double stack — Twins.

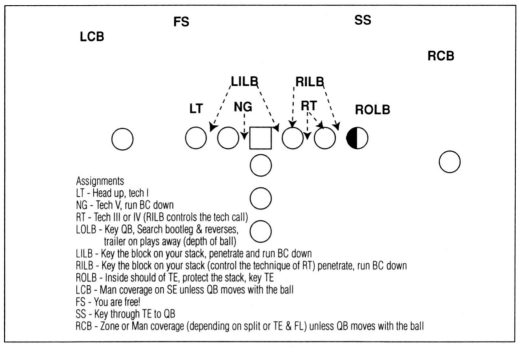

Diagram 6.26. OKIE double stack — 4 deep zone/man.

Assignments
LT - Head up, tech I
NG - Tech V, run BC down
RT - Tech III or IV (RILB controls the tech call)
LOLB - Key QB, Search bootleg & reverses,
trailer on plays away (depth of ball)
LILB - Key the block on your stack, penetrate and run BC down
RILB - Key the block on your stack (control the technique of RT) penetrate, run BC down
ROLB - Inside should of TE, protect the stack, key TE
LCB - Man coverage on SE unless QB moves with the ball
FS - You are free!
SS - Key through TE to QB
RCB - Zone or Man coverage (depending on split or TE & FL) unless QB moves with the ball

DEFENSIVE TEAM PRACTICE

Ninety-five percent of practice on defense should be conducted on a non-contact basis because:

- The larger the number of players involved in a contact session, the greater the chance of someone being injured.
- Since scrimmages tend to be evaluation session more than they are learning and teaching periods, having less contact while scrimmaging tends to increase each player's level of learning and retention of any new material presented.
- In a non-contact scrimmage, more plays can be "fed" to the defense, thereby enhancing the defense's preparation efforts against a specific opponent.
- In most instances, contact is not necessary. Coaches have the option of conducting drills "live" whenever a need for contact arises.

Demonstration (Scout) Team

Most teams employ a demonstration (scout) team to help its defense prepare for a specific opponent/game (whatever it takes). Generally, this group is comprised of young players, new players, and all other substitutes. To a great degree, the better this group is able to maintain their focus and do their job properly, the better prepared the defense will be.

"Feeding" the Defensive Team

One of the most useful techniques to ensure that defensive practice time is well-spent involves taking steps to acquaint the defense with the tendencies and schemes of the opponent's offense. In that regard, the most successful plays of the opponent, with assignments included, should be taken from game videos and drawn-up on play cards the size of regular paper. During practice, the demonstration coaches stand in front of the demonstration team and holds one of these cards high enough so that the team can see their assignments. At the beginning of the week, it might be advisable to "feed" the defense all of an opponent's favorite run plays, then later, all of the passes, and finally the offensive sequences the opponent has shown during recent games. On the last day of full-scale practice, the opponent's trick plays and two-minute offense should be "fed" to the defense. The use of a "demonstration team" can be one of the most effective methods for helping the defensive team prepare for a particular opponent.

CHAPTER 7

RED ZONE DEFENSE

RED ZONE ATTITUDE

Defensive players should maintain their poise and focus and should ascribe to the concept that "since they have not scored yet—don't panic." Defensive players should also be acutely aware of those factors that allowed their opponent to invade the "red zone" and not allow those factors to occur again. For example, the defense must realize that they cannot miss tackles or give less than their very best effort on every play in the red zone.

Once their opponent reaches the red zone, the defense should reflect on their efforts to properly prepare for this particular opponent/game —particularly what steps they should undertake to defend the "red zone." All factors considered, the defense should be better able to defend this area because it encompasses a smaller space than what they have been defending. For example, they should realize passing in this area is more difficult because of the restricted space within the "red zone." At all times, the defense should keep their focus on their "defensive goals":

- To make sure their team does not lose the game.
- To hit hard.
- To make no or few mistakes.
- To not allow first downs.
- To not allow touchdowns.
- To remember that their approach to defending the "red zone" should be an "offensive-oriented defense"; —i.e., hit the gaps; get into the offensive backfield; make plays.

TIGHTEN-UP, LOAD-UP, AND BLITZ

In the red zone, everyone including the secondary, must "squeeze" (tighten up) the line-of-scrimmage. (Refer to Diagram 7.1) In some situations, up to nine men may need to be committed to the run on "running downs" in an effort to "outman" (load-up) the offense or force a pass on those running downs. (Refer to Diagrams 7.2 and 7.3)

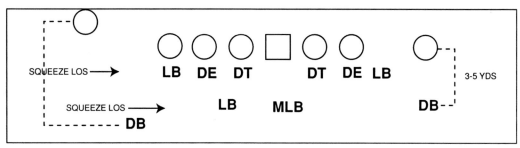

Diagram 7.1. Tighten up the LOS.

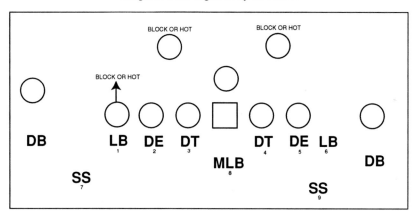

Diagram 7.2. Load up with an even front.

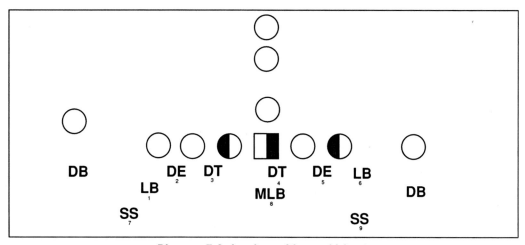

Diagram 7.3. Load up with an odd front.

On passing downs in the red zone, the defense may (and often do) "send players" (blitz) to get to or disrupt the quarterback. If they do, they must take specific steps to cover for the blitz players. One of the goals of a blitzing defense is to try to make the offense throw to "hot" receivers, or make the "hot" receivers stay in to protect the quarterback. Many blitzing teams also cross-charge their defensive linemen to force "switch" blocking by the offensive linemen. Such "switch" blocking may subsequently lead to confusion and/or open lanes to the quarterback. (Refer to Diagram 7.4)

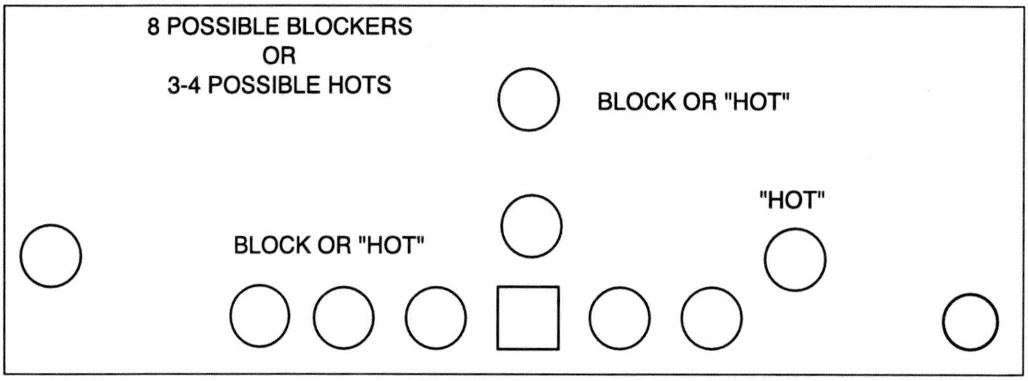

Diagram 7.4. Red zone blitz.

SUGGESTED DEFENSES FROM THE 22-YARD LINE TO THE 10-YARD LINE

Red zone defenses from the 22-yard line to the 10-yard line should be designed to make the opponent "one-dimensional." At that point, the defense can scheme to take away that "dimension". These defenses should be "loaded" against the run. They must also be in a position to put extreme pressure on the passer, while remaining strong at pass coverage. (Refer to Diagrams 7.5 and 7.6)

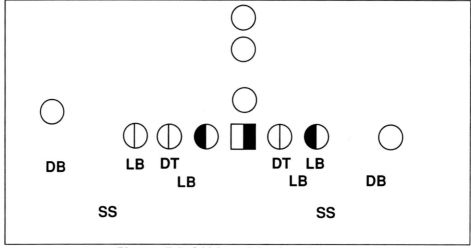

Diagram 7.5. Odd-front defensive alignment.

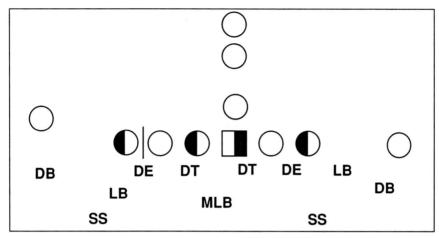

Diagram 7.6. Even-front defensive alignment.

SUGGESTED DEFENSES FROM THE 10-YARD LINE TO THE 4-YARD LINE

Red zone defenses from the 10-yard line to the 4-yard line should be designed to "tighten-up" and "load-up" against the offense by increasing the frequency of defensive linemen moving (angling) into gaps and/or squeezing linebackers into the line-of-scrimmage. (Refer to Diagrams 7.7 and 7.8)

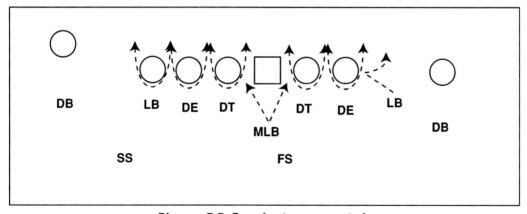

Diagram 7.7. Even-front — gap control.

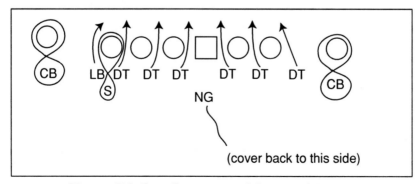

Diagram 7.8. Even-Front— pass defense assignments.

SUGGESTED DEFENSES FROM THE 4-YARD LINE TO THE GOAL LINE

Red zone defenses from the 4-yard line to the goal line should be designed to get gap-penetration by the defensive linemen from either odd or even fronts. (Refer to Diagrams 7.9 and 7.10)

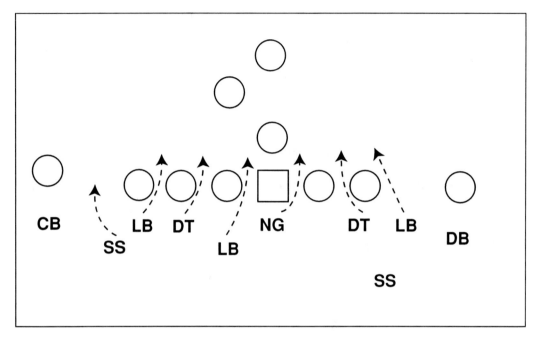

Diagram 7.9. Odd-front defensive alignment.

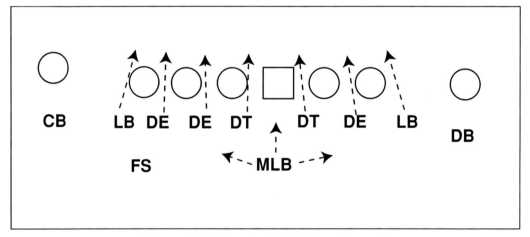

Diagram 7.10. Even-front defensive alignment.

CHAPTER 8

DESIGNING AN EFFECTIVE RUNNING PROGRAM

In recent years, the proliferation of explosive, attacking offenses have placed exceptional demands on defenses. For example, spread offenses with three, four and five receivers, who quickly release into defensive secondaries; shotgun offenses that emphasize no huddles and frequent passing; and offenses that feature speedy backs, who run behind huge, strong, offensive linemen have forced defenses to be better drilled, stronger, more agile, better conditioned, and most of all, faster and more aerobically fit. For example, defensive backs must be able to cover and run with wide receivers for as many as 30- 50 plays a game. Linebackers should be able to run-down speedy backs and cover short, passing areas; and defensive linemen should be able to "stuff" the run, run-down speedy backs, and rush the passer on countless occasions during a game. In order to do all this, defensive players need to be able to "out-run" their offensive counterparts.

Foot speed and aerobic fitness are also important in other aspects of defensive football. For example, special teams players who improve their foot speed and level of aerobic fitness are better able to "cover" kick-returns. Foot speed is obviously an essential trait for kick-returners. Kick blockers should also have the speed required to go after punters and kickers in an effort to block or disrupt their attempts.

Furthermore, every player must be aerobically fit enough so that his heart-lung capacity will enable him to quickly recover from the demands placed upon him during the game. This "recoverability" is crucial to avoid becoming fatigued to a point where his performance is compromised. When players have the pre-requisite foot speed and aerobic fitness they most certainly will elevate the performance level of the defensive and special teams. Accordingly, defensive coaches must be farsighted enough to require all defensive players to regularly engage in speed-work and aerobic workouts. Eventually, these efforts will produce linemen, linebackers and defensive backs who run exceptionally well and who do not become fatigued during the course of a game, and the impact on the performance of the defense will be substantial.

MAKING THE DEFENDERS FASTER

At one time or another, almost every coach has heard clichés such as; "if you're slow, you're slow, if you're fast, you're fast"; "speed kills"; etc. Actually, players who engage in a comprehensive, well-designed speed program will usually become faster. Many coaches believe that each player has a "level of speed", or a "speed threshold", that is determined by that player's weight, strength, and his exposure to speed training (the mechanics involved in the start, stride, body lean, arm action, knee lift, finish).

On the other hand, research and experience have shown that (to a point) a player's level of speed can, in fact, be improved. For example, 40-yard times are measured in relatively small increments (tenths and hundredths of a second). It stands to reason that even small adjustments in a player's body movements, or other minimal changes in an individual's level of fitness can weigh heavily on the 40-yard dash times that a person can achieve. In fact, the speed program outlined and discussed in this chapter has been found to lower the 40-yard times of many football players by as much as 0.5 seconds.

General Ways to Improve Speed:

- Lose weight. When a player is overweight (e.g., overfat), he cannot attain his best "threshold speed."

- Improve the strength of the leg muscles. ("Strong legs run faster than weak legs.").

A Resistance Program for Improving Speed:

- Stretch before and after daily workouts to increase range-of-motion, prepare the body for the demands about to placed upon it, and reduce the likelihood of muscles being pulled. Among the muscles that should be stretched are the hamstrings, gluteus, lower back, groin (adductors and abductors), and the front torso.

- Develop achilles tendon and calf muscles by doing bench jumps daily (start by performing 50 repetitions and then increase the total by five each week). Also perform three sets of squats four times a week with the heels on the floor. Initially, perform the squats with a level of resistance equal to the players body weight minus 20 pounds for 20 repetitions, then his body weight for 15 repetitions; and finally his body weight plus 20 pounds for 10 repetitions. Increase the weight lifted by 20 pounds every three weeks until the player is no longer able to do 10 repetitions at the heaviest weight.

- Work on developing the muscles of the upper thigh, gluteus region, lower abdomen by doing back leg presses (same resistance-level guidelines as for the squats.) Also do knee lifts using a multi-station machine (start the exercise by lifting 10 pounds for 15 repetitions, then 20 pounds for 10 repetitions, and finally 30 pounds for 5 repetitions). Increase the weight lifted by 10 pounds every three weeks until the player is no longer able to lift the heaviest weight five times or the lightest weight 15 times. A third exercise that should be performed is situps or crunches (start with number that "stresses" the player somewhat, and then increase the number of repetitions by five every three weeks).

Speed Training (Running Form):

- Do four-to-six 40-yard sprints at half-speed on the lane lines of a track; focus on achieving and maintaining proper use of arms, knee action, body lean, and running form in general.

- Start by assuming a sprinter's stance and "bunching" the feet in a heel-to-toe alignment (this action minimizes the length of the first step with the rear foot, thus making the first step quicker). Literally, jump out of the stance (for speed). Push-off with both feet, stay low for first few steps, and then slowly raise to a crouch position ("hump" in back), with the body leaning slightly forward. Pump the arms vigorously straight up and down (not across your body as is customary), while trying to increase the speed of this arm-pumping motion.

- Pump the knees high and straight ahead and reach for the ground on each stride, while running on balls of the feet. Run through the finish line. If necessary, lean into the finish line. Run a set of four "gassers", three-to-four days per week (gassers are 220-yard sprints, with resting intervals of 90 seconds between each sprint).

- Run one or two 40-yard sprints for time at the end of each week's work. Keep in mind that timing athletes more often than once a week may slow the player's effort to achieve and sustain proper running form. (Refer to Tables 8-1 and 8-2)

Table 8-1. Recommended times for high school-level gassers.

Down Linemen	First Run	Second Run	Third Run	Fourth Run
220 lbs – 225 lbs	(same as LBs, TE, RBs, QBs)			
225 lbs – 250 lbs	38 sec	41 sec	44 sec	47 sec
250 lbs – 275 lbs	40 sec	43 sec	46 sec	49 sec
275 lbs – 300 lbs	42 sec	45 sec	48 sec	51 sec
LBs, TE, QBs, RBs	36 sec	38 sec	41 sec	44 sec
DBs, WR	33 sec	36 sec	39 sec	41 sec

Table 8.2. Recommended times for college-level gassers.

Down Linemen	First Run	Second Run	Third Run	Fourth Run
225 lbs – 250 lbs	31 sec	33 sec	35 sec	37 sec
250 lbs – 275 lbs	34 sec	36 sec	38 sec	40 sec
275 lbs – 300 lbs	37 sec	39 sec	41 sec	43 sec
300 lbs – 325 lbs	40 sec	42 sec	44 sec	46 sec
LBs, TE, QBs, RBs	29 sec	31 sec	33 sec	35 sec
DBs, WRs	25 sec	27 sec	29 sec	31 sec

A RECOMMENDED RUNNING PROGRAM FOR DEFENSIVE FOOTBALL PLAYERS

The running program presented in this section is based on years of trial and error, using various methods of research, and employing the results of thousands of individual efforts (times). Coaches often ask the question, "Why have a running program for football players, especially defensive football players?" The answer to this issue involves a number of valid, commonsense reasons concerning why a sound running program can be paramount to successful defensive play, including:

- It builds better cardiovascular (aerobic) fitness in players so that, all factors considered, they are more receptive to instruction for longer periods of time. They are also able to give a greater effort for a more extended period of time. As a result, they are less likely to give in to the physical demands placed upon them during a game during the course of a game, and are more likely to be better finishers at the end of games. Once fatigue overtakes a player, he is less likely to retain instructions and more likely to make mistakes.

- It helps players develop a better attitude about their own abilities, because they can now match or overmatch the conditioning level of their opponent.
- It helps players become more disciplined. They know what it feels like to extend, tax, commit to physical activity, experience a high degree of actual physical fatigue, and through it all, reach their goals and be successful.
- It improves the players' level of speed to the extent that they may be able to make plays they previously could not make ("movement is basic to football").
- It helps the players learn that the conditioning derived from a running program is a large part of the "price" (i.e., the commitment) paid by exceptional defensive players and outstanding defensive teams.
- It contributes to the development of mental toughness, a necessary attribute in building powerful defensive teams. A well-designed running program will take participants to the brink of fatigue, and then ask them to "reach down" for more effort. Experiencing fatigue can be a valuable "learning lesson" for players. Coaches should do more than "talk" maximum effort; they should "teach" it.

PREPARING TO RUN FOR TIME

Training and improving the efficiency of a system of the body that is as vital and complex as the cardiovascular system requires both a consistency of routine (discipline) and a willingness to make the necessary time and energy sacrifices to accomplish the desired conditioning goal. Coaches should keep in mind that developing an athlete's level of cardiovascular fitness often takes different lengths of time and effort for each individual. When a coach works with a group of players, he must utilize an exercise regimen that will meet the needs of the "average" player in the group, all-the-while realizing that the routine will be easier for some than for others. Furthermore, the coach should keep his players fully informed about the running program so that they have a clear understanding of what they are being asked to do and why.

Suggested Preparation Routine:

First week – Run seven minutes non-stop, three times per week.

Second week – Run 10 minutes non-stop, three times per week.

Third week – Run 13 minutes non-stop, three times per week.

Fourth week – Run 16 minutes non-stop, three times per week.

Fifth week – Run 19 minutes non-stop, three times per week.

Thereafter – Level off and stay at 19 minutes non-stop, three times per week.

Note: If a player weighs 275 pounds or more, he should run a sixth week at 21 minutes and a seventh week at 25 minutes, and then level-off and stay at 25 minutes. Every runner should be timed once every three weeks to see if he has attained his run-time goal or how near he is to his goal. (Refer to Table 8-3)

Table 8-3. Recommended run times for high school and college-level athletes.

Two-mile run

Down Linemen	High School	College
200 lbs to 225 lbs	(only if the players	same as LBs
225 lbs to 250 lbs	are in a comprehensive	16 min 15 sec
250 lbs to 275 lbs	off-season program)	18 min
275 lbs to 300 lbs		19 min 45 sec
300 lbs to 325 lbs		21 min
325 lbs to 350 lbs		22 min 45 sec
350 lbs to 375 lbs		24 min 30 sec
LBs, TEs, QBs, RBs		15 min 15 sec
DBs, WRs		14 min

One-mile run

Down Linemen	High School	College
200 lbs to 225 lbs	7 min 15 sec	6 min 15 sec
225 lbs to 250 lbs	8 min	7 min 15 sec
250 lbs to 275 lbs	8 min 45 sec	7 min 45 sec
275 lbs to 300 lbs	10 min	8 min 30 sec
300 lbs to 325 lbs	11 min 15 sec	9 min 30 sec
325 lbs to 350 lbs	12 min 30 sec	10 min 45 sec
350 lbs to 375 lbs	13 min 45 sec	12 min 45 sec
LBs, TE, QBs, RBs	7 min 15 sec	6 min 15 sec
DBs, WRs	6 min 45 sec	5 min 30 sec

Quarter-mile run

Down Lineman	High School	College
200 lbs to 225 lbs	90 sec	75 sec
225 lbs to 250 lbs	105 sec	85 sec
250 lbs to 275 lbs	2 min	100 sec
275 lbs to 300 lbs	2 min 20sec	120 sec
300 lbs to 325 lbs	2 min 40sec	2 min 20 sec
325 lbs to 350 lbs	3 min	2 min 40 sec
350 lbs to 375 lbs	3 min 20sec	3 min
LBs, TE, QBs, RBs	77 sec	70 sec
DBs, WRs	70 sec	61 sec

GUIDELINES FOR CONDUCTING TIME TRIALS

After engaging in the aforementioned running training program, every player should be tested in the two-mile run. Once he achieves the recommended time, he should then be tested (as per the recommended schedule for player evaluations) in the one-mile run. If the player is unsuccessful in his efforts to perform the 2-mile run in the prescribed time, he should be tested again in the two-mile run, up to a maximum of five times. At that point, even if he hasn't attained his performance goals, he should then be tested in the one-mile run.

Each player should subsequently be tested in the one-mile run. Once he achieves the recommended time, his quarter-mile run performance should be evaluated. If the player runs the one mile too slowly, he should repeat the one-mile run a maximum of five times. The coach should then have the player move to the quarter-mile run station.

Each player should then be evaluated in the quarter-mile run. If he runs the quarter mile in the recommended time, he then engages in the part of the running program that is devoted to performing gassers. If the player runs the quarter-mile at an unacceptable level, he should be tested two more times on the quarter-mile, before then moving on to the gassers. When the gassers are completed, the running program for that period is concluded.

A significant value exists for a coach to require his players to have their runs timed during the winter off-season, and then timed again immediately prior to spring training. The players should also have their running times assessed during pre-season practice in the fall. In this regard, the coach should strongly encourage his players to condition themselves over the summer in an effort to be ready to be tested. In the process, the players will benefit because they will have shorter periods of time to get out of condition, thereby enhancing their conditioning efforts and making it easier for them to reach their running (aerobic conditioning) goals.

CHAPTER 9

DESIGNING AN EFFECTIVE WEIGHT TRAINING PROGRAM

DISCOVERIES

After years of teaching and conducting research with weight training classes, coaching football players, and studying the weight training efforts of successful football programs across the country, the weight program presented in this chapter was developed. This program has been found to be very well-suited for defensive football players. The following items were discovered from that research:

- Males experience a slight waning of strength about 48 hours after the last resistance exercise session.

- A safe method of determining a "starting point" for how much an individual should lift should be used. An appropriate initial level of resistance is essential if and lifter is to achieve a positive and safe experience in his strength training regimen.

- Repetition-counts and weights tend to be more accurate when the muscle-groups are frequently overloaded.

- Many players can literally "remake" their bodies by engaging in nine- to-12 months of work in the weight room.

- Smaller, weaker, and fewer muscles in a particular muscle group necessitates lighter weights and smaller weight increments between sets.

- The quickest way for a player to improve his performance level on the field is to first get stronger.

- In general, a player's performance improves in direct proportion to his acquisition of strength.

- An individual's nervous system is so complex that it appears impossible to adequately train that system to give back an accurate repetition-count by a once-a-month "max-out" routine.

- The repetition count becomes more accurate by maxing-out at every lifting session.

THE RECOMMENDED PROGRAM

The suggested weight training program for football players involves three basic sets:

- An endurance set— Using a relatively light weight, the purpose of this set is to build muscle endurance (i.e., the ability of the muscle to work over extended periods of time with a minimal expenditure of oxygen and energy).

- A regular set—Employing a somewhat heavier level of resistance, the primary purpose of this type of set is to build muscle endurance, some muscle bulk, and a little muscle strength. As a rule, this set involves lifting 10-20 pounds more than an endurance set, or 10-20 pounds less than an overload set.

- An overload set—Using a relatively heavy weight, the primary purpose of an overload set is to build strength and train the nervous system to adjust to the demands placed on it by the higher level of resistance. This set involves lifting 10-20 pounds more than the regular set. By design, the athlete should not be able to perform very many repetitions of exercise.

Note: Some of the exercises may involve performing four sets instead of three sets. In this instance the purpose would be to provide more work for those muscle groups involved, thus, achieving more muscle bulk. Every athlete should stretch before and after lifting.

LOCATING THE PROPER 'STARTING POINT"

Most weight training programs put an individual through a lot of lifting before locating his starting point on each exercise. In the program outlined in this chapter, a more efficient method of arriving at a starting weight for all of the exercises in this program was determined. This method "cuts through" a lot of lifting to identify the appropriate starting weights. Initially, the procedure involves multiplying the actual body weight of the lifter by a researched percentage. The lifter then lifts this weight as many times as possible, but stops at 15 repetitions if he can perform that many. The point where he stops is his set-weight. The following examples help illustrate the process:

- If the individual lifts a particular weight 15 times, that weight is the amount of resistance he should use for his endurance set. He would then add 10-20 pounds more for his regular set weight, and an additional 10-20 pounds for his overload set weight.
- If the player only lifts a specific weight seven times, that weight would be used for his regular set weight, while that weight minus 10-20 pounds would be his endurance set weight and that weight with 10-20 pounds more would be his overload set weight.
- If the athlete cannot lift the weight a single time, the weight he attempted to lift should be reduced by 10-20 pounds and the exercise performed again. If his "repetition-count" is, hypothetically, three reps, that weight would be his overload set weight. That particular weight down would then be reduced by 10-20 pounds to identify his regular set weight, and lowered yet another 10-20 pounds to serve as his endurance set weight. Therefore, by lifting one set the other two sets can be calculated.

Tables 9-1 to 9-3 provide a list of exercises that should be performed in the recommended weight training program for football players, the number of sets that should be done of each exercise, and a body weight percentage to determine the starting point for a particular exercise.

Table 9-1. Recommended upper-extremity exercises.

Lifts	Sets	Percent of Body Weight
Bench press	4 sets	75%
Military press	4 sets	60%
Incline press	4 sets	60%
Tricep pressdown	3 sets	25%
Lateral pulldown (front & back)	4 sets	40%
Flys (front & lateral)	3 sets	20%
Arm curls (reverse grip)	3 sets	20%
Pullovers	3 sets	20%
Upward angle press	3 sets	50%
High shoulder shrug	3 sets	25%

Table 9-2. Recommended upper- and lower- extremity exercises.

Lifts	Sets	Percent of Body Weight
Power Clean	3 sets	40%
Rowing	3 sets	40%
Bent Leg Dead Lift	3 sets	50%
Good Mornings	3 sets	10%

Table 9-3. Recommended lower- extremity exercises.

Lifts	Sets	Percent of Body Weight
Hip-Leg Press	3 sets	body wt. – 20 lbs
Quarter Squats	3 sets	body wt. – 20 lbs
Leg Extensions	3 sets	10%
Leg Curls	3 sets	10%
Groin Adductors (in & out)	3 sets	10%
Toe Raises	3 sets	body wt. – 20 lbs
Barbell Squats	3 sets	30lbs

INCREASING THE AMOUNT OF WEIGHT LIFTED

The most important factor involved in increasing the amount of resistance that an athlete lifts on a particular exercise is to use a "yardstick" that will enhance safety (i.e., minimize the possibility of muscle tears and strains), while at the same time, will enable the athlete to develop endurance, bulk, and strength. In this regard, the recommended method is repetition-count and time. If the repetition count totals 31 or more for four sets or 24 or more for three sets, the set weight should be increased by 10-20 pounds, whichever increment is appropriate for that particular exercise. By the same token, if the repetition-count is five or more on an overload set, the amount lifted should also be increased.

PROPER LIFTING TECHNIQUES

A few strength training exercises involve some degree of danger because of the specific muscle groups involved in a particular exercise, the order in which they are involved, and the relative level of demands that is placed on a given muscle group as that muscle is being engaged in the exercise. For example, an athlete may pick up a weight with his leg muscles (which are large and relatively strong) and then in the process of transferring that weight to his upper body muscles incorporate his lower back muscles in the exercise (which are only smaller and less strong than the muscles of his legs). Accordingly, an individual should be somewhat cautious when performing quarter squats because of the vulnerability of the lower back to the stress placed on it.

As such, it is extremely critical that every athlete is aware of and adheres to the proper techniques for performing each exercise. For example, strength training exercises involving the musculature of the lower body (e.g., quarter squat, power clean, bent-leg deadlift, barbell squats, toe raises, etc.) should strictly adhere to the following guidelines: avoid ballistic movements (e.g., don't bounce); lift with the legs, not the back; keep the back as straight as possible, and over the hips; keep the head and chin up during the exercise; and avoid placing an under amount of stress on the knees (i.e., don't allow the buttocks to go below the knees while performing an exercise). Each athlete should be encouraged to keep in mind that the primary purpose of strength training is to "build" strength not "demonstrate" it.

LIFTING SESSIONS

During the off-season, an athlete should perform three strength training sessions per week until five weeks before spring training and five weeks before the fall pre-season. At each of these five-week points, the number of workouts should be increased to four times per week. Once the season starts, it is usually appropriate to scale back the number of lifting sessions to two per week (at this point, performing only endurance sets and regular sets). The amount of weight lifted should be increased at the end of each month of the regular season. Tables 9.4 to 9.6 illustrate examples of sheets that players can use to record the results of their strength training efforts. By recording and monitoring their efforts, players will be better able to make whatever adjustments are appropriate in their lifting prescription and routine.

THE LIFTING SEQUENCE

Intense lifting will create an abundance of carbon dioxide and lactic acid (waste) in the muscle tissue. This results in muscle fatigue because the body's reciprocal- innovation process falls behind in removing waste from the bloodstream. In order to reduce or eliminate this blood-chemistry imbalance, it is recommended that the athlete perform one or two upper-extremity lifts initially followed by one or two lower-extremity lifts. This particular lifting sequence enables the athlete to achieve a more valid repetition-count, because while one muscle group works, another rests. Thus, muscle waste build-up tends to be more moderate, thereby allowing the muscles to work harder.

NAME: _____

DATE																							
EXERCISE	SETS	REPS	SETS	REPS	SETS	REPS	SETS	REPS	SETS	REPS	SETS	REPS	SETS	REPS	SETS	REPS	SETS	REPS	SETS	REPS	SETS	REPS	SETS	REPS
Bench Press																								
Military Press																								
Incline Press																								
Lateral Pull Down (F&B)																								
Flys (F&B)																								
Tricep Pressdown																								

Table 9.4. Sample strength training record-keeping sheet.

NAME: _____

DATE																				
EXERCISE	SETS	REPS	SETS	REPS	SETS	REPS	SETS	REPS	SETS	REPS	SETS	REPS	SETS	REPS	SETS	REPS	SETS	REPS	SETS	REPS
Arm curl (reverse grip)																				
Pullover																				
Upward Angle Press																				
High Shoulder Shrug																				
Power Clean																				
Rowing																				
Bent Leg Dead Lift																				

Table 9.5. Sample strength training record-keeping sheet.

NAME _____

DATE																					
EXERCISE	SETS	REPS	SETS	REPS	SETS	REPS	SETS	REPS	SETS	REPS	SETS	REPS	SETS	REPS	SETS	REPS	SETS	REPS	SETS	REPS	SETS	REPS
Good Morning																						
Hip-Leg Press																						
Upward Angle Press																						
Quarter Squat																						
Leg extension																						
Groin Abductor (in & out)																						
Toe Raise																						
Barbell Squat																						
Leg Curl																						

Table 9.6. Sample strength training record-keeping sheet.

CHAPTER 10

THE WINNING EDGE

AN AWESOME RESPONSIBILITY

The Greek philosopher Aristotle once said, "Excellence is not a simple act, but a habit." In this regard, most football coaches are keenly aware that sound habits do not occur by accident. Rather, they are developed over time by paying attention to details and by performing drills on a regular basis. As such, sound habits and strictly adhering to proper technique are the basic foundation of achieving a "winning edge" in football.

Another key factor in achieving the "winning edge" in football involves the fact that the athletes who play on the defensive side of football must be emotionally strong enough to fulfill their basic responsibility (i.e., help their team win the game) on each and every play in each and every game. In order for a coach to inculcate the necessary characteristics and intrinsic attitudes in his players that will enable them to carry out such an awesome responsibility, he should prepare his defensive players through a daily, habit-forming routine that is predicated on:

- The belief that what the coach says is true and must be done in order for the defense to fulfill its specified role.

- The belief that each player should be fully committed to work in the weight room to become as strong as he possibly can be, develop a sufficient level of muscle-bulk to withstand the physical stress imposed on his body during a game, and develop a level of muscle endurance that will allow him to play the game with a unrelenting level of intensity.

- The belief that each player must fully invest his time and energy in a running program that will enable him to become faster, have superior cardiovascular endurance, and develop an attitude that "he in part of a defense that is too mentally tough, too well-conditioned, too strong physically, too fast, and too well prepared for any opponent to beat them."

- The belief, that his players have too much time, effort and physical output invested in the program to ever give anything less than their utmost on every play in every game.
- A belief that the drills that they have performed on a regular basis will provide them with the ability to successfully handle any situation that may arise during the game, and, as such, that they are fully ready to play at all times.

GREAT WORK ETHIC, PLUS GREAT FOCUS, PLUS HIGHLY DRILLED PLAYERS WILL RESULT IN "THE WINNING EDGE"

- Great work ethic:

  Some of the opponents on the schedule might be more talented or larger or smarter or more experienced than your team. However, no opponent should outwork your team during either the season or the off-season in the weight room, in the running program, on the football field.

- Great focus:

  Every player must give his complete attention to the instructions he receives both in the classroom sessions and on the football field. In addition, each player performs his assignments, he must do so with total focus on the proper execution of those assignments.

- Highly drilled players:
- The breaking-down of all assignments into well-designed drills will result in greater acquisition of skills, greater execution of assignments, and fewer assignment mistakes. In other words, great work ethic, plus great focus, plus highly drilled players will provide teams with the "winning edge."

APPENDIX

TERMS

- Anchor – used by outside linebackers on tight ends – linebackers steps into tight end to prevent him blocking either straight ahead or down inside.

- Backdoor – to go around a blocker in an opposite direction of the ballcarrier.

- Backside – the side of the field a way from the formation of an offense.

- Cushion – a distance between a defensive back and a receiver.

- Flatten out – a defensive player braces himself and prevents the blocker from moving him.

- Force man – the perimeter secondary player responsible for defending the wide runs.

- Frontside – the formation side of the offense.

- Hip-pocket technique – to trail a receiver by running directly behind him.

- Pragmatic – practicality determines validity.

- Reps – short for repetitions.

- Ride – forcing a defensive linemen beyond the passer.

- Run under control – running at a speed less than full speed.

- Search – to look for the ball away from the direction of the action.

- Slide the face – to move laterally in front of the blocker.

- Stand-up – to straight-arm shiver an offensive player into a upright position.

- Strongside – the side with the tight end.

- Trash – feet, legs, and bodies of defensive players driven off the line.

- Weakside – similar to backside.

ABOUT THE AUTHOR

A native of Steubenville, Ohio, Joe Gilliam, Sr. is one of the most respected coaches in the history of the game. He began his intercollegiate football career at Indiana University, where he played on the Hoosiers' national championship football team. He then went into the Armed Services, and upon his discharge, enrolled at West Virginia State College, where he played both basketball and football. At West Virginia State College, he received All-American honors as a quarterback and earned a place in the Yellow Jackets' Sports Hall of Fame.

Coach Gilliam began his 35-year coaching career on the high school level in Kentucky, where he earned the Kentucky High School Football Association's Coach of the Year title. He went on to coach on the collegiate level at Jackson State College in Mississippi, helping lead the Tigers to two National Black Football Championship titles.

From 1963-1981, Gilliam was the assistant head football coach and defensive coordinator for Tennessee State University. In 1989, he took the helm as head coach for four seasons. During this time, he was inducted into the TSU Sports Hall of Fame, and was selected as Coach of the Year in the Ohio Valley Conference in 1990. His illustrious career record of 254-93-15 included coaching five undefeated teams and five other teams that lost only one game. In the process, he coached ten teams to national championships, and helped guide 144 players into professional football careers with the National Football League. Most recently, he worked with the Arizona Cardinals' coaching staff as an offensive consultant during the summer.

Throughout his extensive career, Gilliam has earned numerous awards, including the All-American Football Foundation Lifetime Achievement Award and the College Football Hall of Fame Contribution Award. A frequent guest speaker and sought-after lecturer at football clinics, radio programs and sports banquets, he is widely renowned for the ability of his teams to employ his innovative coaching concepts and insights.